Contents

Welcome!

Welcome! We're so excited that you have decided to pick up this book and give some of the cocktails inside a try. Making delicious mixed drinks at home doesn't have to be a daunting task. We are passionate about the fact that great cocktails can be made by anyone, anywhere, with minimal fuss, equipment or specialist knowledge. In following our simple guidelines, we hope to empower you to have more fun with flavour, learn new techniques and, above all, make amazing cocktails that you and your friends can enjoy.

How This Book Works

The concept of *60-Second Cocktails* is really all about fun and flavour exploration. It's centred on the positive belief that, with a little practice and preparation, anyone can make a terrific mixed drink in roughly the time it takes to select, open and pour a bottle of wine. Within these pages you'll find 60 different cocktails, some of them original recipes as well as a number of tasty twists on classics that you might already be familiar with. We've broken these down into three distinct groups, which vary in complexity and style:

CHAPTER 1:
NO SHAKE, SHERLOCK

First up are 20 fun, more everyday-style cocktails that don't require much preparation, equipment or anything other than a few key storecupboard ingredients – you'll find a list of what we recommend you keep at hand on pages 14–15.

CHAPTER 2:
SHAKE IT UP

Next comes a selection of 20 drinks that will need a good ol' shake, stir or perhaps the odd additional piece of equipment or ingredient.

CHAPTER 3:
MAGNIFICENT MIXES

We finish with 20 cocktails that call for a few specialist ingredients and a little more preparation, adding to their sophisticated flavours and complexity.

All our cocktail recipes make a single drink to serve one person, unless where we've said otherwise. And with each cocktail recipe you'll find the following...

NAME & DESCRIPTION

Cocktails, like kids and cars, are often given names, and we've done the same here, along with a short description of the drink to help bring to life the liquid in the glass.

INGREDIENTS LIST

The components of the mixed drink that you'll need to get out and prepare in advance – make sure you have all your bottles open and your juices freshly squeezed!

WHICH GLASS?

This is not prescriptive. Try experimenting with different styles, shapes and sizes. And it's a good idea to chill your chosen glass in readiness – see page 13 for more on that.

WHAT ABOUT A GARNISH?

Most of the drinks need a great looking/smelling/tasting garnish, so try to prepare it in advance – see page 21 for a few tips and tricks.

WHAT EQUIPMENT WILL I NEED?

Rest assured, there's nothing too complicated here – mostly a means of measuring the ingredients, something to mix them in, or a cocktail shaker, and a strainer.

DO I ADD ICE?

There are different sorts of ice, from small cubes to blocks and crushed, and different ways of using them in cocktail making, so here we tell you if, what and how it's best used.

HOW DO I MAKE THIS?

A brief description of how best to bring the drink together.

NON-ALCOHOLIC OR LOW ABV

Planning on drinking very little alcohol or none? We've included a few low-ABV (1.2% or less) or non-alcoholic serves at the end of each chapter, if you fancy something lighter.

GOOD FOR BATCHING

In a few cases, we'll recommend that a drink can be made in a larger batch and stored for later – especially useful if you have a few guests coming over.

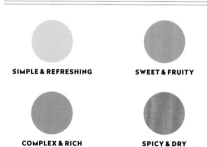

SIMPLE & REFRESHING · SWEET & FRUITY

COMPLEX & RICH · SPICY & DRY

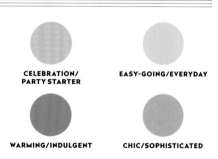

CELEBRATION/PARTY STARTER · EASY-GOING/EVERYDAY

WARMING/INDULGENT · CHIC/SOPHISTICATED

FLAVOUR GROUP

We've tried to break each drink down to fit into a certain flavour group, which can be useful when preparing for a get-together, or simply deciding on a type of food it might pair well with.

OCCASION SUGGESTION

This is to show when each drink will dazzle the most. Some are crackers to open the weekend with, others are simple drinks you can enjoy at any time. Then there are a few that are perfect for the 'wow' factor if you're entertaining, or just for a bit of quality 'me/we' time.

Key Cocktail Kit

The tools you'll need as well as items that can be improvised

Walk into any decent cocktail joint and you'll see a huge array of gadgets behind the bar designed to help the staff mix up their drinks in the best possible way. It can be somewhat mind-boggling for the average drinker seeing all the different mixing jars, muddlers, measures, shakers and whatnot all neatly lined up, constantly being washed and replaced ready to use again. And watching the bartenders at work can seem as smooth-yet-complex an operation as a Formula One pit stop.

There are some absolute essentials that you'll need when it comes to mixing up great cocktails at home. But you don't need the whole range of gear to get the ball rolling in making awesome mixed drinks, and there are plenty of shortcuts or alternative items you can use to achieve the same results.

MEASURE

This is the most vital piece of kit in your cocktail-making armoury, for measuring out each liquid that is going into the mix. Why? Because cocktails are all about balance, and it's this balance that helps you walk the tightrope between a good drink and a great drink.

Most bars use a jigger measure, which looks like a metal egg timer, normally with one larger end that holds 50ml of liquid and the other smaller end holding 25ml. Most cocktail books give measures in millilitres (ml) or fluid ounces (fl oz), or both, but since we are all about ease here, we use 'parts', where 1 part = 25ml (1fl oz). This means that you don't need a professional measure at all, just a smallish receptacle that allows you to measure liquid out consistently. An egg cup is ideal, or a shot glass, both of which hold roughly 50ml (2fl oz). So if a recipe asks for, say, 2 parts vodka and 1 part espresso coffee, then use one full egg cup or shot glass of vodka and half an egg cup or shot glass of coffee. Simple, eh!

1 PART
=
25ML / 1FL OZ

COCKTAIL SHAKER

On the whole, a cocktail shaker is key to making a mixed drink – but not essential, as our first group of cocktail recipes shows. There are two main types of cocktail shaker:

Boston Shaker

This consists of two halves, one metal and one glass, one slightly bigger than the other so that they fit perfectly together. A separate strainer is required for this style of shaker (see below).

Cobbler Shaker

This looks a little like a New York fire hydrant and comes in three parts, often all metal: a large compartment for ingredients, a lid with a built-in strainer and a cap that frequently doubles as a 1-part measure (see page 6).

However, maybe you're visiting a friend and want to mix up a cocktail but you're stuck for a shaker, in which case you can use a number of alternatives. We have been known to shake up a mean Sour using a Kilner jar or even whip up an Espresso Martini in a sports water bottle! Whatever item you improvise with, it's vital that it's not too fragile and can be sealed closed so that it's watertight.

STRAINER

Nearly all drinks made in either a cocktail shaker or a mixing glass (see page 8) will need to be strained, holding back the ice and any other bits and pieces that were added to impart flavour from your serving glass. The advantage of using a Cobbler shaker is that your strainer will be built in, but if using a Boston shaker or when straining drinks from a mixing glass, you'll need a cocktail strainer, sometimes called a Hawthorne, to cover one half of the shaker or the mixing glass top as you pour out the mixture.

'Fine straining' is a term reserved for drinks that are double strained – passed through the standard cocktail strainer and also a tea strainer or small fine sieve. Using something other than a cocktail shaker? Just strain through a regular kitchen sieve or large tea strainer into the glass.

CITRUS SQUEEZER

You may well already own some sort of citrus squeezer or juicer, but if you don't, we really recommend you opt for a handled citrus squeezer, where you place a citrus fruit half in the nook by the hinge (often called the 'Elbow'), close it, squeeze hard and hey presto – juice! However, people commonly make the same mistake using this citrus squeezer as they do with a wetsuit: they use it backwards. As the zip on a wetsuit goes at the back, so the fruit half goes into the dimple of the citrus squeezer upside down, like a dome. As the other half of the squeezer presses down on the fruit, it pushes it inside out and releases all the goodness within.

An electric juicer, should you have one, comes in handy for pre-juicing a large batch of citrus fruit when required or if you're making several of the same cocktail. No shame in using a little technology here!

MIXING GLASS

This allows you to stir a drink with ice, diluting it as you do so. But you don't really need a special bit of kit here – in fact, two of the world's best bars, Swift in London and Little Red Door in Paris, use small, flat-sided stainless-steel storage containers from a well-known Swedish store. If they can, so can you!

MUDDLER

A large wooden stick, reminiscent of a miniature Victorian rolling pin, the muddler's job is to crush down ingredients such as fresh herbs and citrus fruit to release their flavours before mixing and/or shaking. You can use the end of a small rolling pin that fits inside your cocktail shaker or glass instead.

BAR SPOON

Pretty much what it says on the tin, this is a small spoon with a long shaft to allow you to stir your cocktails and reach all the way to the bottom of the glass, to where a lot of the heavier ingredients sink. This will help to give your drink a much better consistency. The spoon itself contains about 5ml (1 teaspoon), so is ideal for adding precise amounts of a flavoursome ingredient for perfect balance. Many bar spoons have a twisted shaft, around which you can curl a narrow ribbon of citrus peel for a more flamboyant garnish (see page 22).

VEGETABLE PEELER

Many of our cocktails call for a thin piece of citrus peel as a garnish, for which you need a vegetable peeler to cut the outer peel of the fruit (see page 22).

KNIFE & CHOPPING BOARD

The thing about citrus fruit is that they come whole, so you'll need a good-quality, sharp knife (careful, now!) along with a sturdy, non-slip chopping board to halve them for squeezing and to cut them up for garnishes (see page 22).

... AND FRIENDS

Finally, the best drinking accessory is your friends. Okay, not a cabinet essential (occasionally a bit of solace and a Whisky Sour is what we need in life), but drinking together is nearly always better than drinking alone.

Glassware Gems

The crystal clear vessels that make your drinks sing!

The phrase 'we eat and drink with our eyes' may not win you any points with those who focus solely on flavour, but there's no denying that the right kind of visual aesthetic can have a huge influence on how we perceive whether we'll like or dislike a drink. Presenting a brilliantly made Old-Fashioned in a chipped and faded novelty coffee mug that your granny bought you for Christmas a decade ago might serve a practical purpose, but it's unlikely to give off that air of love, care and attention that you've worked hard to put into making its contents.

So while you don't need to be hurrying along to an expensive artisan Venetian glass blower, it's well worth planning ahead to see what gaps might exist in your glassware cupboard, and which items might be resurrected from the attic and dusted off.

It's also here that you can start to bring an element of personalization to your drinks. Some of the best glasses we've ever used have been second-hand, sourced from charity shops, car boot sales and antiques shops. Vintage and retro glasses might mean you don't have a complete set of the same style, but when the only thing your guests are talking about is how great the drink looks and tastes, who cares!

COUPE: THE CLASSIC COCKTAIL GLASS

Often seen in 1920s-themed Art Deco movies, the coupe is the personification of sophisticated elegance. It's sometimes associated with Champagne (more on that in a second), but its shallow-yet-wide, voluptuous curves and thin stem give any shaken, stirred and strained cocktail such as the Martini, Manhattan, Daiquiri, Gibson or Gimlet that feeling of ultimate timeless indulgence and refinement. These days, coupes are much more widely available, with many mainstream glassmakers offering a terrific, dishwasher-safe version. The key is to buy the sort that aren't going to break the bank if you do accidentally drop one on the floor, and also to get a moderately sized version rather than a gigantic fishbowl because, let's face it, there's not a lot right with a glass that looks half empty.

THE V-SHAPED COCKTAIL GLASS

Hugely popular, this is often called a Martini glass and bears a resemblance to the coupe. While not quite as visually exciting, there's nothing wrong with serving a classic drink in one of these. However, as with the coupe, keep an eye on the glass size. If you're making a Martini in a large one, the quantity will need to be humongous and consequently the drink will be very boozy and difficult to keep chilled. We really love the smaller-sized versions – the Nick & Nora is the ideal, similar to a small wine glass in capacity but with that classic, slightly flat-sided look and thin stem.

THE ROCKS GLASS

An absolute must, the rocks glass, or short tumbler, can take many forms and styles, but the principle is the same: a short, heavy-based glass, either uniformly cylindrical or with cut-glass sides. It's the perfect vessel for the likes of the Old-Fashioned (see pages 52 and 130), Negroni (see page 48) and other shorter drinks that are served 'on the rocks' – over ice cubes. Some glasses are straight-sided and are ideal for larger single pieces of ice, whereas some angle in a little and favour smaller cubes, which will melt faster and dilute the drink more quickly.

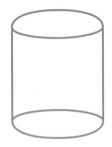

THE HIGHBALL GLASS

This is the glass to build your tall, effervescent drinks in. Anything using sparkling water or another mixer always looks great in a highball. They're usually narrower in diameter than a rocks glass, so might not suit a huge block of ice, but filled to the brim with smaller cubes, a garnish and a straw, they're fantastically summery and presentable.

THE FLUTE

Now commonly known as a Champagne glass (replacing the coupe, which you can often see in vintage pictures of precariously balanced Champagne towers), with its delicate, tall and slender sides, long stem and small base, the flute is perfect for any aperitif cocktail and lighter, more celebratory drinks. We again recommend finding moderately sized ones that aren't too fragile, as your drink will go further in them and you can give them a quick stir to re-fizz the frothy head without fear of damaging the glass.

THE BOWL, OR COPA GLASS

A new kid on the block, the copa, or bowl, or Gin & Tonic balloon, has become very popular with gin drinkers internationally. They were arguably first used in Spain a decade ago, where the modern-day fascination with gin really took hold and bartenders began to look for new, dramatic ways to present their Gin & Tonics, giving them room for loads of ice cubes, plenty of tonic and perhaps the odd gin botanical thrown in for good measure alongside the traditional garnish. The copa is great for spritzes and seltzers, but don't forget that it holds a lot of liquid, so you'll need to fill it with ice to make it look good. If your cabinet is already pretty full, you can't go wrong with a large, wide-brimmed wine glass, which effectively does the same thing.

A SHOT GLASS

Fairly self-explanatory, this is a useful glass to have in your cabinet, even if you don't use it for shooting! As mentioned earlier, most shot glasses hold a double measure, or '2 parts' in the measures we use in our recipes, making it a handy alternative to a jigger. Occasionally you'll see them accompany another glass, as in some Martinis that come with a side order of Prosecco to mix into the main drink.

OTHER VESSELS TO EXPLORE

Once you have established your glassware cabinet essentials, it's worth looking for a few unusual 'statement' pieces that can add extra theatre to certain drinks, especially anything that has a theme or a signature ingredient. You'll discover in the recipes that we have experimented with a vintage teacup and saucer and a wide-brimmed coffee cup; a Hurricane glass – a cross between a bowl, a highball and a large wine glass, which is great for punches and rum-based drinks; a metal camping mug, which can bring a touch of the outdoors in, or vice versa; and an old friend, rescued from the attic, a stainless-steel goblet bought from a junk shop in South London.

FROM THE PROS

◆

Although this book is about making quick, easy and tasty drinks, there's nothing wrong with a bit of pre-prep and one of the best tips with your glasses is to pre-chill them in the freezer first, before pouring a drink into them. Not only will it help keep the drink cooler for longer, it will add a wonderful frosted look to the drink and build the anticipation of the drinker! Just be careful with chilling super-thin glasses: you don't want to end up breaking them, which sudden temperature changes can bring on.

Your Home Bar

The basic ingredients you need to get started

The backdrop to any high-end cocktail bar is a kaleidoscope of colourful bottles. These are often supported by a mysterious collection of miniature vessels in varying shapes, usually with distinguished-looking labels. Some may even have vaguely scientific-like dropper pipettes for measuring out minute quantities of the potent elixirs inside.

There will also be a selection of bottles hidden from the customer's view but within easy reach of the bartender, known as the 'speed rail', as these are the most often used and form the foundation of the majority of cocktails, including sugar syrup, bitters and of course all the standard spirits.

When putting together your own home bar, you don't need to aim for a comprehensive range of booze bottles, but there are some absolute essentials in which we have rooted many of the cocktails in our first two sections of recipes. What are these can't-live-without bottles that every cocktail fan should have at hand? Read on to find out.

Spirits

The basic spirits that any home bar should have to recreate the cocktails in this book are as follows:

VODKA

The simplest of all distilled drinks in as much as it is designed to be colourless and flavourless. This doesn't, however, mean that the drinks it makes are in any way lacking. Vodka brings a whack of alcohol to any mixed drink, and we would always encourage the use of one with a minimum of 40% ABV (alcohol by volume), but no higher than 46% ABV. For the sake of balance, ensure the vodka you choose is not too 'funky' or flavoured but clean, crisp and neutral in style.

WHISK(E)Y

A wide category (but not as wide as rum!), these same six (or seven) letters cover everything from super-smoky single malt Scotch to bold bourbon from America and incredibly smooth Irish whiskey. We have tried to be a bit more specific in our recipes, narrowing down what's required for each drink into:

American Whiskey

Anything made in the USA, such as Jim Beam, Jack Daniel's, Maker's Mark or Woodford Reserve. These are rich, sweet whiskeys, with strong flavours and aromas of fresh vanilla and cherries. Some higher-end bourbon whiskey can be very high in ABV (or proof), so try to avoid those; around 40% ABV (80 proof) is ideal.

Irish Whiskey

This is lighter and more floral in style than American whiskey. Think brands such as Jameson and Bushmills.

Scotch Whisky

We divide this into two camps: smoky and non-smoky. The best way to tell the difference is with a quick sniff – if the whisky smells of barbecue or bonfires, you have a smoky Scotch on your hands. Both single malt and blended Scotch are acceptable to use in cocktails. Ignore those who say that single malt can't be mixed – it can and your drink will be all the better for it!

GIN

Gin is basically vodka flavoured with juniper berries and other botanicals (such as spices, herbs, roots, bark and fruits). There is nothing wrong with the big brands you see in the supermarkets that have been around for centuries. They have survived this long because they are great! Our advice is to use a London Dry gin (the gold standard for gin production) and try and choose one with an ABV between 40% and 48%. Pink

gin has been post-flavoured with ingredients that have a vibrant pink colour, such as strawberry or rhubarb. Sloe gin, a gin-based fruit liqueur, is also a great bottle to have in your collection, being sweet and fruity in taste and rich red in colour.

TEQUILA

A drink some folk might have had a bad experience with in the past, tequila is one of the most flavoursome of all spirits, with a totally unique taste. We advise you to seek out anything labelled '100% agave', otherwise there is a risk it is a tequila adulterated with other ingredients. Tequila can be coloured, known as 'gold', 'oro' or 'joven', but try and stick to 100% agave silver (blanco) tequila, or those that are darker in colour and labelled añejo (aged) or reposado (rested).

RUM

Probably offering the widest spectrum of flavour of any spirit, rum is made from molasses or sugar cane and can mostly be found in white, spiced or dark styles. Dark rum can simply be white rum with colouring added, so look for one that has spent some time resting in an oak cask.

Warning: as some spiced rums can be very low in strength, ensure you choose one that is at least 35% ABV.

BRANDY

Brandy is distilled from wine or fermented fruit juice and aged in oak casks. The most famous types of brandy, produced in specific regions of France, are Cognac, Armagnac and Calvados. The first two are made from grapes and when we call for 'French Brandy', either Cognac, Armagnac or another French Grape Brandy can be used. When we ask for the orchard fruits-based Calvados, we will make this clear.

OUR RECOMMENDED SELECTION

- vodka
- American, Irish and non-smoky Scotch whisk(e)y
- London Dry gin
- 100% agave silver (blanco) tequila
- white, aged dark and spiced rum
- French brandy

Wines, Liqueurs, Beers & Other Essentials

A good home bar should also have a few other key bottles in order to make a decent selection of mixed drinks, as follows:

VERMOUTH

Vermouth is wine that has been fortified (had some spirit added to it) and flavoured with herbs and spices. It is essential to have a bottle of both dry vermouth and sweet vermouth.

SHERRY & PORT

Sherry (from Spain) and port (from Portugal) are fortified wines that range from dry to spicy, nutty and sweet in style. We have featured various types in our recipes, including dry fino or manzanilla and rich, nutty oloroso sherries, as well as fruity ruby port and drier, more complex tawny port. But as our recipes have been designed to work with most styles, a bottle of any port and any sherry would be fine.

TRIPLE SEC OR CURAÇAO

A sweet, colourless liqueur flavoured with orange. Famous examples are Cointreau and Grand Marnier.

CHERRY BRANDY LIQUEUR

A dark, seductive drink that will add colour, sweetness and fruity flavour to your cocktails.

SPARKLING WINE

A number of our recipes call for a bit of fizz to add some desirable sparkle! Sparkling wine is produced all over the world, the most famous examples being Champagne (France), Prosecco (Italy) and Cava (Spain). We'll leave it up to you which one you choose, although we make a few specific suggestions.

BEERS

We have used beer in a few of our recipes. One calls for a stout – a dark beer such as Guinness, another features a white wheat beer and two ask for a fruity IPA. These beers each bring specific and unique flavours to their respective cocktails.

FRUIT JUICES

Most cocktails need some form of citrus or fruit, not just to make them tasty but also to bring some acidity to the drink and balance out the sweetness. Lemon and lime juices should be freshly squeezed (see page 22), and orange juice can be, too, but it's okay to use shop-bought ready-prepared orange juice in cartons. Pineapple, tomato and apple juices can also be shop-bought. Passion fruits are cut in half and the contents scooped out for use in drinks.

COCKTAIL BITTERS

The equivalent of salt and pepper in cooking, bitters are practically indispensable in making cocktails. They add small explosions of highly intense flavour and come in a huge variety of styles: from chocolate to chilli, and orange to black walnut. We recommend that any home bar should have a bottle of standard Angostura bitters (with a yellow lid) and the orange version from the same company (with an orange lid). See page 25 for how to make your very own bitters.

SUGAR SYRUP

Almost every cocktail needs an element of sweetness, often delivered by sugar in the form of a syrup. While you can buy ready-made sugar syrup in most supermarkets, it's just as easy to make your own, so see pages 24–5 for recipes for standard simple sugar syrup plus several different flavour variations.

OUR RECOMMENDED SELECTION

◆ dry and sweet vermouth
◆ sherry
◆ port
◆ triple sec or curaçao
◆ cherry brandy liqueur
◆ sparkling wine
◆ lemons, limes and oranges (see page 22)
◆ apple and pineapple juice
◆ Angostura bitters – standard and orange
◆ sugar syrup (see page 24 for homemade)

Mixers

TONIC WATER

The last few years have seen a huge growth in tonic water brands, and flavoured tonic water, too. We would recommend using standard tonic water when required in the recipes.

SPARKLING WATER

You can use shop-bought sparkling water or soda water, or make it at home using a carbonating machine such as SodaStream.

GINGER ALE & GINGER BEER

These are very different, ginger ale being lighter in style, while ginger beer is spicier and cloudy.

APPLE SODA & LEMONADE

Apple soda can be shop-bought (Appletiser is a good example) or made using apple juice and sparkling water. Lemonade is any sparkling lemon juice drink, such as Lemon Fanta. Any standard lemonade can be used.

OUR RECOMMENDED SELECTION

◆ tonic water
◆ sparkling water
◆ ginger ale and ginger beer

We always recommend keeping a supply of small cans of these ready to use, to ensure the drinks remain fresh and fizzy. The last thing you want to hear is a depressingly faint 'pphhffff' as you unscrew the bottle top!

EVERYDAY KITCHEN INGREDIENTS

Egg white is used in mixed drinks to give them a silky texture and to add a frothy head, so don't forget your eggs! No need to waste the yolk – keep in the refrigerator to use in cooking. For those drinkers who are vegan or wish to avoid eating raw egg, there are various effective alternatives, such as aquafaba, the liquid from canned chickpeas, which we call out in our recipes.

Our cocktails also draw on a range of items we believe would be standard in most kitchens, including: Tabasco and Worcestershire sauces, balsamic vinegar, extra virgin olive oil, beef stock cubes, various jams, preserves and marmalade, honey, maple syrup, chocolate hazelnut spread, peanut butter, canned peaches and pineapple, black peppercorns for cracking and grinding, fresh chilli, ground cinnamon and cinnamon sticks, whole nutmeg for grating, drinking chocolate powder, teas, espresso coffee (from a pod coffee machine), almond milk, blackcurrant and elderflower cordials, desiccated coconut, coconut cream, vanilla and chocolate ice creams and lemon sorbet.

Some Speciality Ingredients

To add a little pizzazz to your drinks

Armed with the essential ingredients itemized in the previous pages, you'll be in good shape to make most of the cocktails in this book. But we have let our creativity run a bit more wild in the final section of recipes, so they require some ingredients you may have to buy in specially.

ABSINTHE

A famous drink, often known as 'the green fairy', with a strong flavour of herbs, especially aniseed.

CALVADOS

A brandy made in France from apples and sometimes pears as well (see page 15).

CHAMBORD

A French raspberry liqueur.

GINGER LIQUEUR

Sweet and full of ginger flavour. A good example is The King's Ginger.

MEZCAL

Another popular Mexican spirit from the same family as tequila (see page 15). It tends to be more earthy and carry a distinct smoky note that tequila doesn't have.

OTHER BITTERS

There are some different styles of bitters called for in certain recipes including Peychaud's (see page 126), black walnut bitters (see pages 142 and 152) and chocolate bitters (see pages 130, 132 and 144), so look out for them and order them up in advance.

Bartender Tips & Techniques

To get you shimmyin' and shakin'

If there's one sage piece of advice we've picked up from the professional bartenders we know, it's about being as best prepared as possible: line up everything that you possibly need in advance of making your drinks. This is especially vital if you're only giving yourself a short amount of time to make your drink! Also – though this might sound obvious – keep it clean, baby! Having a dry tea towel to hand is essential – you'll manage to keep hold of that slippery, wet cocktail shaker a lot longer and won't be cleaning sticky Daiquiri off your kitchen cabinets. In addition to these bartender bible basics, here we look at a few useful tips to help you prepare your drinks efficiently and make them look absolutely stunning.

Ice

THE most important party guest

There's a saying we pretty much live by when having friends over: 'You run out of ice, you run out of party!' There's not a lot worse than going to the trouble of preparing all your cocktail ingredients, then heading to the freezer to find an ancient plastic ice-cube tray with only a couple of cubes, so always plan ahead. If you're using an ice-cube tray, try to keep refilling it as many times as possible and then transferring the ice cubes to sealed freezer-proof containers or resealable freezer bags to bring out for the big event. If you're planning to buy in bags of ice, always opt for solid cubes, not the cylindrical ones with holes in, as they melt almost straight away and you'll quickly end up with a very watery drink.

MAKING CRUSHED ICE

It's pretty simple. Fill a sturdy ziplock plastic bag with ice cubes, wrap a tea towel around it and place on a work surface or the floor. Whack it with a rolling pin for 30 seconds or so. But be careful not to reduce the ice to slush – tiny pieces are perfect!

MAKING YOUR OWN 'BAR-STYLE' ICE BLOCKS

A large chunk or block of ice is great for bringing out the best in a cocktail like a Negroni (see page 48), as it will take longer to melt and dilute the drink and looks more elegant. Simply find yourself a sturdy plastic straight-sided food storage box and fill with freshly boiled filtered water that has been left to go cold. Freeze and you should end up with a nice, clear block, which you can then carefully break into smaller pieces using a sharp knife or ice pick.

HOW MUCH ICE?

Lots! A great drink will benefit from plenty of ice, remain cold for longer and look infinitely better than just slinging in a couple of tiny cubes. Use ice straight from the freezer rather than leaving it out to go wet. Always use ice cubes in a cocktail shaker, not crushed ice or blocks, and never reuse the ice from the shaker in your serving glass: keep it fresh and fabulous.

OTHER WAYS TO CHILL

In addition to chilling your glassware in the refrigerator before use (see page 13), it's also worth turning some of your refrigerator shelf space over to a few key bottles if you have room. Items such as port, sherry and vermouth will quickly start to lose their freshness once opened unless kept sealed in the refrigerator.

Shaking

HOW TO SHAKE

Don't be fooled! There is no wrong or right way to shake a cocktail. So long as the vessel you choose is given a rigorous, chilly agitation for about 5–10 seconds, you'll be fine. One important point is to check if you shake the drink with ice, or initially without, known as the 'dry shake', which is used to help build up a creamy foam, before you finish shaking the cocktail with ice added to the shaker. A good tip is to fine strain (see page 7) shaken drinks when serving them 'straight up', i.e. not poured over ice, in order to filter out any little shards of ice, which can dilute the drink further and don't look great floating around in an attractive glass!

A vital piece of advice is to keep your hands firmly on the lid and always shake away from your guests – the last thing they need is an emergency trip to hospital before they can enjoy their cocktail! And when pouring the drink, keep hold of all the pieces of the shaker and strainer, or risk becoming a viral YouTube clip, as the lid catastrophically falls into the drink, knocking it all over the kitchen counter or dinner table (yes, we're guilty as charged).

SHAKEN VS STIRRED COCKTAILS: WHAT WOULD BOND SAY?!

Put simply, shaking a drink with ice allows you to chill it quickly with only minimal dilution from the melted ice. Stirring a drink with ice in a mixing glass gives you greater dilution from the melted ice to reduce the cocktail to a more drinkable alcoholic strength, while also chilling the drink. Some spirits and ingredients are a little heavier or more viscous than others, so when mixing them together, try to use a folding action – a bit like folding a cake mixture – rather than just moving them around in a circular fashion, to lift and integrate them more thoroughly.

In our opinion, some classic cocktails, like the Manhattan and Classic Martini, actually benefit from being stirred rather than shaken, giving a much more enjoyable, balanced and smooth-tasting drink. So sorry, Mr Bond, we'll have to agree to disagree on this one!

Garnishes

The lowdown on the high point of your cocktail

The garnish in any cocktail serves two purposes. First, it helps lift the look and feel of the drink, giving colour and some texture to the liquid in the glass. Second, and perhaps more importantly, a garnish can really bring crucial scented top notes and refreshing, zesty or herbal aromas to the drink, helping to highlight the spirit or other ingredients in the cocktail. As well as drinking with our mouths, let's not neglect our good old noses! The most popular are citrus slices and peels, each different variety helping to bring something unique to the party.

Try to prepare your garnishes before you make your cocktails – it will give you more time to concentrate on the business of mixing a masterpiece.

FRESH CITRUS SLICES & WEDGES

These add tangy, juicy, fruity flavours to a drink, and you can nibble on them, too. When cutting a citrus slice or wheel, always cut vertically down into the fruit from the middle to create a 5mm (¼-inch) slice, to show it off in the best light. For wedges, cut along the length of the whole fruit to halve it and then slice each half into quarters, or eighths in the case of larger fruits.

CITRUS PEELS

The outer peel of citrus fruit contains a lot of tasty oils that, when 'expressed' over the surface of the finished drink, deliver a wonderful burst of aroma and fresh flavour. Citrus peels also look superbly professional when cut properly and are easy to prepare, if you give yourself enough time. Always choose fresh citrus fruits, which will be packed with aromatic oils. First, give your fruit a little wash and a scrub with a kitchen brush to remove any dirt or wax. Then take a vegetable peeler and cut from the top to the bottom of the fruit to create a long, elegant slice. Next, using a sharp knife running flat to the back of the peel, carefully remove as much of the white pith as possible without breaking the peel, to avoid introducing unwanted bitter flavours into the drink.

To express the oils, hold a piece of the prepared peel over the glass, skin side down in the middle between the thumb and forefinger of each hand, and squeeze the long edges together to leave an oily sheen on the drink's surface. Then simply slip the peel into the glass to complete the look.

You can also trim and shape your peel, and here the sky's the limit! Try trimming the edges with crinkle-cut scissors for a zigzag effect, or cut the peel into a diamond shape. You can also use your sharp knife to cut a small slit down the middle of the peel, allowing you to place it on the rim of the glass.

To create a long spiral, cut around the circumference of the fruit with the peeler to create as long a piece of peel as possible, then remove the pith as above and carefully trim down to a narrow ribbon, like a lace. Then wrap it around the (often twisted) shaft of a bar spoon to give it an impressive coiled spring-like effect.

All citrus peels can be pre-prepared and stored for up to 5–6 hours before making your cocktails. Place them in an airtight food storage container with a piece of moistened kitchen paper in the bottom and refrigerate.

DRIED CITRUS WHEELS

These add a refined crystallized visual appeal to a drink and are easy to make in advance and store. Preheat your oven to 70°C (160°F). Line a baking tray with nonstick baking paper and set a wire rack on top. Slice your citrus fruit into thin wheels (the thinner, the quicker they will dry out) and lay them on the rack, then place in the oven to dry. Lemon and lime wheels will take about 4–5 hours, whereas orange wheels (particularly juicier blood oranges) can take 6–7 hours.

Take out of the oven and leave until completely dry, fully cooled and brittle to the touch before removing from the rack. They can be carefully stored between sheets of kitchen paper in an airtight container in a cool, dry place for up to around 6 months.

ORCHARD FRUITS

Orchard fruits, such as apples and pears, bring a fabulous, sweet, perfumed aroma to a cocktail and taste delicious, too. A couple of our drinks call for apple slices as a garnish, but if you want to get really creative, why not make an apple fan. Cut down one side of a medium-sized apple so that you have a perfect round slice free of any core or pips, then make three or four cuts in the cheek to divide it into slices but stopping just short of the base, to avoid separating the slices. With care, fan out the slices at the top and use to garnish your drink.

FRESH HERBS, CHILLI & CUCUMBER

If you're using mint or other fresh herbs such as sage, basil, rosemary or thyme as a garnish, give the leaves a gentle slap between your palms, or roll on the kitchen counter, to release the fresh aromas into the drink. You can also gently heat the leaves of tougher fresh herbs like sage or rosemary in a pan to help open up their aroma. And most of these herbs can be kept as pot plants, giving you a plentiful supply of fresh garnishes. Drinks like the Mojito (see our Tequito, page 60) and Mint Julep (see our Wondermint Julep, page 92) need plenty of fresh mint to make them really sing. When muddling mint in the bottom of the cocktail shaker, the aim of the game is simply to release as much minty goodness, flavour and aroma as possible, so it doesn't need to be mashed to pieces!

The humble cucumber is a great cocktail ingredient, and to create an elegant accompanying garnish, use your vegetable peeler to remove the skin down one side of the cucumber and then to cut a long, wide ribbon from its length (see Cucumber Cooler, page 108).

A slice cut from a fresh red chilli makes a suitably vibrant garnish for a feisty cocktail (see Firecracker Margarita, page 74).

Techniques

FOAM ART

If, like us, you've always been hugely impressed by the way coffee baristas serve up devilishly attractive-looking lattes and cappuccinos, you'll be pleased to hear that you can also bring a couple of such artistic flourishes to your cocktails. If you're making a cocktail that has a wonderfully creamy foam top, such as The Big Apple on page 100 or The Classic Whiskey Sour on page 86, add a few carefully placed drops of bitters on to the foam and use a cocktail stick to sketch out a pattern for a truly professional finish. Also, when adding a dusting of chocolate powder, ground cinnamon or grated nutmeg to your foam top, try covering half with a small piece of card as a mask, to create a clean line down the centre.

Sensational Homemade Ingredients

Recipes for adding a little magic of your own

Alongside your assembled arsenal of shop-bought spirits and other cocktail ingredients, it's well worth exploring a few twists and turns of your own making. Taking a personal spin on a mixed drink can bring about something completely unique and potentially – you never know – a classic cocktail of the future! So here are a few recipes to get you started.

Syrups & Purées

Sugar syrup is the core ingredient of a huge number of cocktails, from the Old-Fashioned to the Mojito, but in addition to the obvious sweetness, it can add nutty, malty flavour by using different types of sugar. Many of the recipes in the book call for only ½ part sugar syrup, which is equal to 12.5ml or 2¼ teaspoons, so a little goes a long way! Once made, you can store any of these sugar syrups in a sterilized airtight bottle or jar in the refrigerator for up to 3 months.

SIMPLE SUGAR SYRUP
+ **Makes approx. 400ml (14fl oz)**

We find the ideal ratio of sugar to water here to be 2 parts sugar to 1 part water. Add 300g (10½oz) white caster sugar to a saucepan and cover with 150ml (5fl oz) water. Gently heat, being careful not to bring to the boil, and stir until you have a clear, silky syrup. Let it cool completely before spooning off any foamy residue from the surface, then strain into your sterilized bottle or jar, seal and store.

MUSCOVADO SUGAR SYRUP
+ **Makes approx. 350ml (12fl oz)**

This is a nuttier, more indulgent syrup, and because muscovado sugar is darker and richer, we have slightly reduced the amount of sugar in relation to the water. Add 250g (9oz) light muscovado sugar to a saucepan and cover with 150ml (5fl oz) water. Heat until bubbling, then reduce the heat and stir until all the lumps have disappeared. Cool completely, spoon off any foamy residue and bottle and store as for the simple syrup.

RASPBERRY PURÉE
+ **Makes approx. 250ml (9fl oz)**

Add 200g (7oz) fresh

raspberries to a blender with 25ml (1fl oz) water and blitz until smooth. Stir in 50ml (2fl oz) simple sugar syrup or, for a richer style, muscovado sugar syrup (see opposite for homemade), then strain through a fine sieve into a small jug to remove the seeds. Cover with clingfilm and store for up to 5 days in the refrigerator. You can make a strawberry purée in the same way, but use only 25ml (1fl oz) sugar syrup.

SPICED SUGAR SYRUP
✦ **Makes approx. 200ml (7fl oz)**
A wintery, warming syrup. Add 150g (5½oz) demerara sugar, 100g (3½oz) raisins, the peel of 1 lemon and ½ orange (washed), 1 teaspoon cloves, 1 teaspoon ground ginger, 1 star anise and 1 cinnamon stick to a saucepan with 100ml (3½fl oz) water. Boil, then simmer for 8 minutes. Let cool completely, then strain through a fine tea strainer into a sterilized bottle or jar.

SMOKY CHOCOLATE SYRUP
✦ **Makes approx. 200ml (7fl oz)**
A truly heavenly combination! Add 150g (5½oz) white caster sugar, 4–6 teaspoons dark drinking chocolate powder and 100ml (3½fl oz) strongly brewed lapsang souchong tea (using 2 teabags) to a saucepan. Bring to a gentle boil and stir, then take off the heat and leave to cool. Spoon off any foamy residue from the surface, strain into a sterilized bottle and store as before.

Bitters

As mentioned earlier, bitters are one of the most important ingredients in a huge variety of cocktails, often referred to as the 'seasoning element'. While you'll probably only really ever need one bottle of Angostura bitters in your cabinet (it seems to last a lifetime!), it's also worth exploring a couple of recipes of your own, using the following as a template. Try experimenting with other spices from your storecupboard, such as coriander seeds or vanilla pods, or smoky lapsang souchong tea or dried fruit.

KITCHEN CUPBOARD BITTERS
✦ **Makes approx. 50ml (2fl oz)**
You'll need a bottle of standard vodka and a selection of botanicals: cinnamon sticks, cloves, star anise, cardamon pods, black peppercorns and lemon peel. Also clean several small airtight jars, to which you add 100ml (3½fl oz) vodka per 5g (⅛oz) botanical, keeping each different botanical to a separate jar. Then wait for the magic to happen. Lighter botanicals, such as lemon peel, give up their flavour more quickly, whereas the harder,

woody ones like star anise can take longer. Our rule of thumb is to check them regularly and after 2 weeks you'll probably get the results you're looking for. Once you're happy with the flavours and aromas, you can start to add small amounts of each infusion to a bottle or separate jar as your final blend. Begin with the more dry, earthy flavours like the cinnamon and star anise, then build your blend with the rest, finishing with the black pepper. When it comes to cardamom, a little goes a long way, so watch out for this little green meanie!

Index of Recipes

by main spirit or ingredient

Have a scan through to find your favourite spirit or headline ingredient, and perhaps use this as a starting point to dive in. Some of the drinks, such as the New Orleans Legend and Cincuenta/Cincuenta, include equal measures of other wines, beers and spirits, too, but we've listed them by what we regard as *the* defining ingredient.

Gin

Brandy

Vodka

Wine

Whisk(e)y

Rum

Tequila & Mezcal

Other

No Shake, Sherlock

Easy, everyday stunners that need
minimal preparation and only a few ingredients

Easy-Peasy Paloma

A classic Mexican cocktail with a magical mix of silver (*blanco*) tequila, citrus notes and effervescent soda. The original calls for grapefruit soda, but you can use a lemonade for a more rounded and sweet citrusy punch. You can alternatively use a blood orange soda.

- 1 part silver (*blanco*) tequila
- squeeze of fresh lime juice
- 5 parts pink grapefruit soda

WHICH GLASS?

A highball or other tall glass.

WHAT ABOUT A GARNISH?

A fresh grapefruit slice – pink grapefruit looks fabulous!

WHAT EQUIPMENT WILL I NEED?

A jigger measure and bar spoon.

DO I ADD ICE?

Yes, fill the glass to the top with ice cubes.

HOW DO I MAKE THIS?

Add the ice to the glass, then add the tequila and lime juice and top up with the soda. Give the drink a quick stir with the bar spoon and garnish with the grapefruit slice.

SIMPLE & REFRESHING   EASY-GOING/EVERYDAY

Quick Sloe Gin & Soda

Sloe gin is a marvellous concoction – a combination of fresh and fragrant ripe berry aromas with a hint of sharpness and dryness coming from the juniper and other gin botanicals. Simply lengthening it with sparkling water leads to a long, fruity and seriously refreshing drink.

- ◆ 2 parts sloe gin, such as Sipsmith or Elephant
- ◆ 5 parts sparkling water

WHICH GLASS?

A highball or other tall glass.

WHAT ABOUT A GARNISH?

A fresh orange slice.

WHAT EQUIPMENT WILL I NEED?

A jigger measure and bar spoon.

DO I ADD ICE?

Yes, fill the glass to the top with ice cubes.

HOW DO I MAKE THIS?

Add the ice to the glass, then add the sloe gin and top up with the sparkling water. Give the drink a quick stir with the bar spoon and garnish with the orange slice.

SIMPLE & REFRESHING   EASY-GOING/EVERYDAY

Splendid Sherry Seltzer

Looking for a wonderful, refreshing way to revitalize that leftover sherry?
Well, this is it! Whether it's the drier style fino (which we use here) or
manzanilla, the slightly more complex and darker oloroso, Bristol cream, or even
the sticky-sweet, rich Pedro Ximénez, sherry makes a terrific concentrated base
for a deliciously simple long drink.

◆ 3 parts sherry – for a drier
drink, use fino or manzanilla,
or for a richer, nuttier result,
try oloroso

◆ 5 parts tonic water

WHICH GLASS?

A large wine glass.

WHAT ABOUT A GARNISH?

A thin piece of lemon peel.

WHAT EQUIPMENT WILL I NEED?

A jigger measure
and bar spoon.

DO I ADD ICE?

Yes, works wonderfully
with a few large ice cubes
or an ice block.

HOW DO I MAKE THIS?

Add the ice to the glass, pour
over the sherry and then
slowly pour in the tonic water.
Squeeze the lemon peel over
the top of the drink to express
the oils (see page 22) and add
to the glass to garnish.

SIMPLE & REFRESHING   CELEBRATION/PARTY STARTER

Douro Spritz

This drink comes from a wonderful trip we took to Porto in
Northern Portugal and takes its name from the majestic Douro Valley,
the heartland of port production. It plays very much on the aperitivo hour –
that superbly chilled time where you take a moment to enliven the
senses before dinner, truly waking up the taste buds!

- ◆ 3 parts fruity ruby port – or for a drier, richer drink, use tawny port
- ◆ 1 dash freshly squeezed lemon juice
- ◆ 1 dash sparkling water
- ◆ 3 parts sparkling wine, such as Prosecco – or for a low-ABV version, use 1 dash sparkling wine and 3 parts sparkling water instead

WHICH GLASS?

A large wine glass.

WHAT ABOUT A GARNISH?

A fresh or dried orange slice.

WHAT EQUIPMENT WILL I NEED?

A jigger measure
and bar spoon.

DO I ADD ICE?

Yes, plenty of ice cubes.

HOW DO I MAKE THIS?

Add the port and lemon juice
to the glass, then add the ice
and sparkling water. Top up
with the sparkling wine. Stir
a few times with the bar spoon
and garnish with the
orange slice.

SWEET & FRUITY   CELEBRATION/PARTY STARTER

Temple Bar Cooler

Irish whiskey (blended or single malt) is a great way to explore a lighter, fruitier style of whiskey. Brands such as Jameson or Bushmills work really well in a long drink, and the freshness of the whiskey is highlighted here by the zinginess of apple soda and a touch of spice from the bitters.

- ◆ 2 parts Irish whiskey
- ◆ 2 dashes Angostura bitters
- ◆ 4 parts apple soda, such as Appletiser

WHICH GLASS?

A tall highball glass.

WHAT ABOUT A GARNISH?

A fresh green apple slice.

WHAT EQUIPMENT WILL I NEED?

A jigger measure and bar spoon.

DO I ADD ICE?

Yes, fill the glass to the top with ice cubes.

HOW DO I MAKE THIS?

Add the whiskey and bitters to the glass and quickly stir with the bar spoon. Then add the ice and the apple soda. Stir several times again and garnish with the apple slice.

SIMPLE & REFRESHING   CELEBRATION/PARTY STARTER

Wicked Whisky Highball

The whisky highball is currently topping the charts around the world as the most fashionable bar call. A refreshing mix of a great blended Scotch such as Johnnie Walker Black Label and sparkling water, this is a great way to drink whisky. The addition of cracked black pepper to the top of the drink accentuates the smoky notes.

- 2 parts Scotch whisky – blended works perfectly here
- 5 parts sparkling water
- sprinkling of freshly cracked black pepper (optional)

WHICH GLASS?

A tall highball glass.

WHAT ABOUT A GARNISH?

A thin piece of lemon peel.

WHAT EQUIPMENT WILL I NEED?

A jigger measure and bar spoon.

DO I ADD ICE?

Yes, fill the glass to the top with ice cubes.

HOW DO I MAKE THIS?

Add the ice to the glass and then the whisky, giving a few stirs with the bar spoon to wake up the whisky. Add the sparkling water and, if you like, sprinkle the cracked black pepper on top of the drink. Stir again 7–8 times and squeeze the lemon peel over the top of the drink to express the oils (see page 22) before adding to the glass to garnish.

SIMPLE & REFRESHING   EASY-GOING/EVERYDAY

Spiced Rum & Pineapple Fizz

Rum is famed for being an easy-to-drink spirit, and a dark and spicy version goes really well with fruity flavours, especially pineapple.

- ◆ 2 parts spiced rum, such as Captain Morgan or Kraken
  - ◆ 2 parts pineapple juice
- ◆ squeeze of fresh lime juice
- ◆ 4 parts sparkling water

WHICH GLASS?

A tall highball glass.

WHAT ABOUT A GARNISH?

A fresh lime wedge.

WHAT EQUIPMENT WILL I NEED?

A jigger measure and bar spoon.

DO I ADD ICE?

Yes, fill the glass to the top with ice cubes.

HOW DO I MAKE THIS?

Add the spiced rum, pineapple juice and lime juice to the glass, then add the ice. Stir quickly with the bar spoon, then top up with the sparkling water. Add the lime wedge to garnish and stir again a few times.

SWEET & FRUITY   CELEBRATION/PARTY STARTER

Super Sonic

The Gin & Tonic is a cracking drink that, when made with a bit of care and attention, is possibly the most refreshing long drink in the world. But wait, there's an alternative to this classic! The Super Sonic takes refreshment to a new level, rolling back the natural bittersweet notes of tonic by bringing in sparkling water as the main mixer and results in a drink that is lower in sugar than a normal G&T.

◆ **2 parts London Dry gin**
◆ **4 parts sparkling water**
◆ **2 parts tonic water**

WHICH GLASS?

A tall highball glass.

WHAT ABOUT A GARNISH?

This one is up to you – try experimenting! We love a fresh lime wedge, but equally, a fresh pink grapefruit or lemon slice works well.

WHAT EQUIPMENT WILL I NEED?

A jigger measure and bar spoon.

DO I ADD ICE?

Yes, fill the glass up to the top with ice cubes. Don't hold back!

HOW DO I MAKE THIS?

Add the ice to the glass, then the gin and give a little stir with the bar spoon. Carefully add the sparkling water and stir again, then add the tonic water to the top. Garnish with the lime wedge or your chosen citrus slice.

SIMPLE & REFRESHING   EASY-GOING/EVERYDAY

The Berliner

After many years in the doldrums, shandy is well and truly back, and this is our supremely easy take on it, mixing German *Weissbier* with apple soda. Who knew apple and beer could work so well together! For additional flavour, try adding a couple of dashes of Angostura bitters.

- ◆ 2 parts *Weissbier* – or any available white wheat beer
- ◆ 1 part apple soda, such as Appletiser

WHICH GLASS?

A chilled beer glass.

WHAT ABOUT A GARNISH?

None needed.

WHAT EQUIPMENT WILL I NEED?

A jigger measure and bar spoon.

DO I ADD ICE?

None needed.

HOW DO I MAKE THIS?

Carefully pour the beer into the glass, then slowly pour in the apple soda. Give a quick stir with the bar spoon, but watch that the resulting head doesn't get too big for the glass!

SIMPLE & REFRESHING   EASY-GOING/EVERYDAY

Next Level Negroni

Complex in flavour yet simple to make and arguably one of the cocktail world's most inspired creations, no wonder the classic Negroni has become an international favourite over the last few years. It's a drink that allows your choice of gin to shine through and will give you many flavoursome avenues to explore. We've tweaked the formula slightly for an extra fruity version. For a completely different twist, swap out the gin entirely and use a bourbon or fruity Scotch whisky to create a Boulevardier.

- ◆ 1 part **London Dry gin**
- ◆ 1 part **Campari**
- ◆ 1½ parts **sweet vermouth**

WHICH GLASS?

A rocks glass or short tumbler.

WHAT ABOUT A GARNISH?

A fresh orange slice or a dried orange wheel.

WHAT EQUIPMENT WILL I NEED?

A jigger measure and bar spoon.

DO I ADD ICE?

Yes, a large ice block works best, but a few large cubes will be fine, too.

HOW DO I MAKE THIS?

Add the ice to the glass, then pour over the gin, Campari and sweet vermouth. Stir with the bar spoon for about 8–10 seconds, then garnish with the orange slice or dried orange wheel.

SPICY & DRY

CHIC/SOPHISTICATED

GOOD FOR BATCHING

Gi-Gi

A spicy, warming mixed gin drink, based on the classic
Mule cocktail. Perfect for the chilly autumnal or winter months,
leaving your taste buds tingling.

- 1 part London Dry gin
- 2 dashes Angostura bitters
- 5 parts ginger ale
- squeeze of fresh lime juice

WHICH GLASS?

A large wine glass.

WHAT ABOUT A GARNISH?

A fresh lime wedge.

WHAT EQUIPMENT WILL I NEED?

A jigger measure
and bar spoon.

DO I ADD ICE?

Yes, plenty of small ice cubes.

HOW DO I MAKE THIS?

Add the gin, bitters and ice to
the glass and give a quick stir
with the bar spoon, then top
up with the ginger ale. Add
the lime juice, stir again a few
times and garnish with the
lime wedge.

SPICY & DRY

WARMING/INDULGENT

Maple Syrup Old-Fashioned

A tasty twist on the classic Old-Fashioned, this uses American whiskey and gets its complex sweet and slightly smoky flavour from the addition of maple syrup. Traditionally, the Old-Fashioned takes a little time to prepare, but we're cheating a bit here. Try experimenting with different styles of sugar syrup (see page 24 for homemade) and other bitters – you can't really go wrong!

- 2 parts American whiskey, such as Jack Daniel's or Maker's Mark
- ½ part maple syrup
- 2 dashes Angostura bitters
- 1 dash cold water

WHICH GLASS?

A rocks glass or short tumbler.

WHAT ABOUT A GARNISH?

A thin piece of orange peel.

WHAT EQUIPMENT WILL I NEED?

A jigger measure and bar spoon.

DO I ADD ICE?

A large ice cube looks great, but a few decent-sized cubes will help to dilute and chill the drink.

HOW DO I MAKE THIS?

Add the whiskey, maple syrup and bitters to the glass, then a dash of cold water. Stir for around 20 seconds with the bar spoon, then add a little ice. Give a final stir, then squeeze the orange peel over the drink to express the oils (see page 22) and place on top to garnish.

COMPLEX & RICH   CHIC/SOPHISTICATED   GOOD FOR BATCHING

Homemade Hard Seltzer

Arguably one of the world's biggest recent drinks trends, the hard seltzer is a lighter take on a sparkling water serve. Ideal for outdoor gatherings, barbecues and picnics, here's a dead simple way to make your own at home.

- ◆ 1 part vodka
- ◆ ½–1 teaspoon seedless fruit preserve, such as cherry, apricot, raspberry or strawberry
- ◆ 5 parts sparkling water

WHICH GLASS?

A highball glass.

WHAT ABOUT A GARNISH?

A fresh basil leaf or cucumber slice.

WHAT EQUIPMENT WILL I NEED?

A jigger measure, teaspoon and bar spoon.

DO I ADD ICE?

Yes, fill the glass to the top with ice cubes.

HOW DO I MAKE THIS?

Add the vodka and preserve of your choice to the glass and stir with the bar spoon until you have a smooth consistency. Add the ice and sparkling water and stir vigorously for a few seconds until thoroughly mixed. Give the basil leaf a gentle slap between your palms to release the aroma and place on top of the ice to garnish, or just add the cucumber slice.

SIMPLE & REFRESHING   EASY-GOING/EVERYDAY

Bloody Maria

As weekend brunch drinks go, the Bloody Mary is pretty much unbeatable, with the savoury/spicy combo pairing perfectly with everything from croissants to the humble fry-up. However, swapping out the traditional vodka for silver (*blanco*) tequila switches up the drink into something even more spectacular. Our recipe brings in a touch of meatiness, too, to keep you going until dinnertime!

- ◆ **2 parts silver (*blanco*) tequila**
- ◆ **½ beef stock cube**
- ◆ **2 dashes Tabasco sauce**
- ◆ **3 dashes Worcestershire sauce**
- ◆ **grind of black pepper**
- ◆ **5 parts tomato juice**

WHICH GLASS?

A glass mug or large highball glass.

WHAT ABOUT A GARNISH?

A fresh lemon wedge and two cherry tomatoes, skewered on a cocktail stick.

WHAT EQUIPMENT WILL I NEED?

A jigger measure and bar spoon.

DO I ADD ICE?

Yes, fill the glass to the top with ice cubes.

HOW DO I MAKE THIS?

Add the tequila to the mug or glass, crumble in the stock cube and stir with the bar spoon until roughly dissolved. Then add the Tabasco, Worcestershire sauce and black pepper. Add the ice, then top up with the tomato juice. Give the drink a final quick stir to mix everything together and add the garnish.

SPICY & DRY   EASY-GOING/EVERYDAY

Tropical Twister

Two of the tastiest rum drinks are the simple Dark 'n' Stormy and the fruity Hurricane. This cocktail is the eye of the storm – the point where these two classics cross over, bringing together zesty citrus fruit, spicy ginger and vibrant tropical rum notes. The perfect drink for warm days and sultry evenings.

- ◆ 1 part white rum
- ◆ 1 part dark rum
- ◆ 1 part pineapple juice
- ◆ 3 parts ginger beer
- ◆ ½ part freshly squeezed lime juice
- ◆ 1 dash Angostura bitters

WHICH GLASS?

A Hurricane glass or tall highball glass.

WHAT ABOUT A GARNISH?

A fresh pineapple slice or lime wedge, or both!

WHAT EQUIPMENT WILL I NEED?

A jigger measure and bar spoon.

DO I ADD ICE?

Yes, fill the glass to the top with ice cubes.

HOW DO I MAKE THIS?

Simply add the ice to the glass, then all the ingredients and stir with the bar spoon, folding together and lifting until well mixed. Garnish with the pineapple slice and/ or lime wedge.

SWEET & FRUITY

WARMING/INDULGENT

Tequito

The Mojito is one of the most beloved cocktails in the world and one of the easiest to make. Our take on it adds a Mexican flair to the proceedings by switching out the rum for temptingly tasty silver (*blanco*) tequila. The result is a crisp and sweet combo of wonderfully refreshing flavours.

- 1 part silver (*blanco*) tequila
  - 1 teaspoon simple sugar syrup (see page 24 for homemade)
- squeeze of fresh lime juice
- handful of fresh mint leaves
  - 4 parts sparkling water

WHICH GLASS?

A tall highball glass.

WHAT ABOUT A GARNISH?

A sprig of fresh mint.

WHAT EQUIPMENT WILL I NEED?

A jigger measure, teaspoon, muddler and bar spoon.

DO I ADD ICE?

Yes, fill the glass to the top with ice cubes.

HOW DO I MAKE THIS?

Add the tequila, sugar syrup, lime juice and mint leaves to the glass. Crush the mint with the muddler for about 10 seconds to release the flavour. Add the ice, top up with the sparkling water and stir with the bar spoon for a few seconds. Garnish with the sprig of mint.

SWEET & FRUITY

CELEBRATION/PARTY STARTER

Affogato Snowstorm

Affogato, the classico Italian dessert of vanilla ice cream and espresso coffee, is perhaps the perfect way to end a meal. This cocktail version combines the added punch of a shot of vodka and the spice of Angostura bitters. Grab a spoon and get stuck in!

- ◆ 1 scoop vanilla ice cream
- ◆ 1 part vodka
- ◆ 2–3 dashes Angostura bitters
- ◆ 2 parts freshly brewed hot espresso coffee
- ◆ 1 teaspoon desiccated coconut

WHICH GLASS?

A wide-brimmed coffee cup works perfectly, with a spoon.

WHAT ABOUT A GARNISH?

None needed, but we found this little skiing chap who fancied his chances off-piste!

WHAT EQUIPMENT WILL I NEED?

A jigger measure and teaspoon.

DO I ADD ICE?

None needed.

HOW DO I MAKE THIS?

Add the ice cream to the cup and pour over the vodka. Add the bitters to the coffee and then pour into the cup. Sprinkle over the desiccated coconut and serve with a spoon to eat it with.

COMPLEX & RICH

WARMING/INDULGENT

Hot Peanut Butter Rum

Dark rum is a spirit full of complexity and works brilliantly in a number of mixed drinks that call for big, rich flavours. Hot Buttered Rum is a hugely underrated classic cocktail and we've given it a twist by using smooth peanut butter, which adds an indulgent, silky element of nuttiness.

- 2 parts dark rum
- 2 teaspoons clear honey, first loosened with a little warm water
- 1 teaspoon smooth peanut butter
- 4–5 parts hot, but not boiling water

WHICH GLASS?

Grab your favourite mug and fill her up!

WHAT ABOUT A GARNISH?

None needed, but a piece of peanut brittle to munch on pairs wonderfully well.

WHAT EQUIPMENT WILL I NEED?

A jigger measure, teaspoon, separate jug for mixing and tea strainer.

DO I ADD ICE?

No! Keep it piping hot, baby!

HOW DO I MAKE THIS?

Add the rum and honey to the jug and mix with the teaspoon until the honey has fully dissolved. Add the peanut butter, pour over a little of the hot water and stir until melted. Pour in the remaining hot water and give a last quick stir, then strain through the tea strainer into your mug.

COMPLEX & RICH   WARMING/INDULGENT   GOOD FOR BATCHING

The Ultimate Champagne Cocktail

Using sparkling wine, particularly Champagne, elevates any cocktail to another level of decadence and sophistication. This bona fide classic is one of the most impressive party drinks and is devilishly easy drinking, with a delicate floral note and rich sweetness. We've jazzed it up by using muscovado sugar syrup for extra complexity, but why not try our other sugar syrup recipes (see pages 24–25)!

- 1 part brandy – Cognac is the classic choice, but any good, fruity brandy will do
- ½ part muscovado sugar syrup (see page 24 for homemade)
- 3 parts well-chilled Champagne or other sparkling wine
- 2 dashes Angostura bitters

WHICH GLASS?

A flute.

WHAT ABOUT A GARNISH?

A spiral of lemon peel.

WHAT EQUIPMENT WILL I NEED?

A jigger measure and bar spoon.

DO I ADD ICE?

None needed, but ensure the sparkling wine is cold from the refrigerator and chill the glass in the freezer beforehand (see page 13).

HOW DO I MAKE THIS?

Add the brandy and sugar syrup to the glass and give a quick stir with the bar spoon to mix. Then carefully add the sparkling wine, leaving a little room at the top. Add the bitters and gently stir until frothy. Garnish with the spiral of lemon peel, with a little dangling from the glass.

SWEET & FRUITY

CELEBRATION/PARTY STARTER

Temperance Tea

The number of great non-alcoholic spirit alternatives available in most major supermarkets means that there are plenty of delicious bespoke drinks to be mixed up for anyone who fancies a night off the sauce. This Temperance Tea pays a cheeky homage to the roaring 1920s Prohibition, when drinkers concealed their cocktails in teacups.

- ♦ 1 part non-alcoholic or low-ABV botanical spirit, such as Seedlip or Portobello Road Temperance
- ♦ ½ part clear honey, first loosened with a little warm water
- ♦ 4 parts chilled green tea

WHICH GLASS?

A teacup, ideally a nice porcelain one, with a saucer.

WHAT ABOUT A GARNISH?

A fresh lemon slice.

WHAT EQUIPMENT WILL I NEED?

A jigger measure and bar spoon.

DO I ADD ICE?

None needed.

HOW DO I MAKE THIS?

Add the botanical spirit and honey to the teacup and mix with the bar spoon until the honey has fully dissolved. Add the chilled green tea and then give the lemon slice a little squeeze over the drink before adding it to the teacup to garnish.

SIMPLE & REFRESHING   EASY-GOING/EVERYDAY   GOOD FOR BATCHING

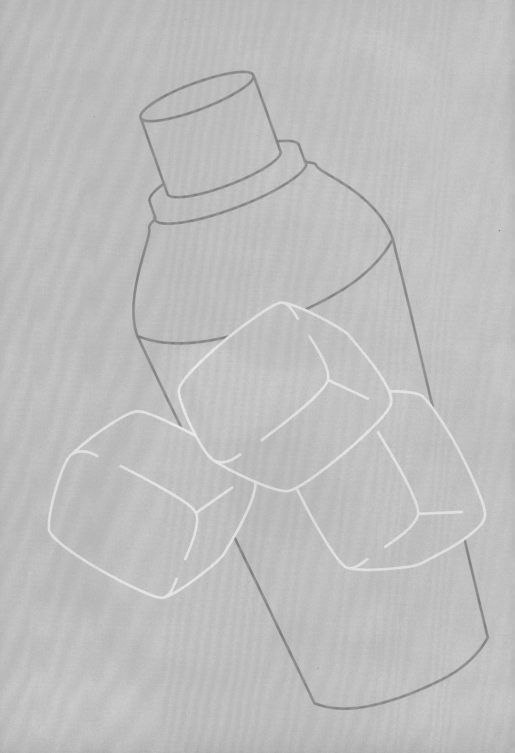

Shake
It Up

Slightly more complex concoctions
that need a quick shake or stir

Brilliant Bellini

One of the most enduring classics of all time, the Bellini is about as Italian chic as it gets, famously conceived in Venice at Harry's Bar, one of Humphrey Bogart's and Ernest Hemingway's favourite hangouts back in the 1950s. It brings together peach purée, exploding with floral freshness, and crisp sparkling Prosecco. The addition of raspberries gives this mix a beautiful hue as well as lifting the taste.

- ♦ 125g (4½oz) drained canned peaches
- ♦ handful of fresh raspberries
- ♦ 1 part cold water
- ♦ 4 parts chilled Prosecco or other sparkling wine

WHICH GLASS?

A flute.

WHAT ABOUT A GARNISH?

Two fresh raspberries.

WHAT EQUIPMENT WILL I NEED?

A blender, jigger measure, tablespoon and bar spoon.

DO I ADD ICE?

None needed.

HOW DO I MAKE THIS?

Add the peaches, raspberries and water to the blender and blend until slightly puréed. Add a large tablespoon of the purée to the glass and then the chilled sparkling wine. Gently fold together, lifting and stirring with the bar spoon. Garnish with the raspberries.

SWEET & FRUITY   CELEBRATION/PARTY STARTER   GOOD FOR BATCHING

Firecracker Margarita

The Margarita is pretty much THE perfect drink as it is, and can be served 'straight up' (without ice) or over ice cubes or crushed ice. Versatile and delicious, our take on it adds a touch of spice to give it a real Mexican kick. The devil – or *el diablo* – is in the detail with the amount of heat you add to this bad-boy-of-a-cocktail.

- ◆ 2 parts silver (*blanco*) tequila
- ◆ 1 part freshly squeezed lime juice
- ◆ 1 part triple sec
- ◆ ½ part simple sugar syrup (see page 24 for homemade)
- ◆ 1 dash Tabasco sauce (or more if you're a daredevil!)

WHICH GLASS?

A rocks glass or short tumbler, or you can strain the drink into a coupe if you like.

WHAT ABOUT A GARNISH?

Fresh red chillies and a fresh lime wheel.

WHAT EQUIPMENT WILL I NEED?

A jigger measure and cocktail shaker and strainer.

DO I ADD ICE?

Add ice cubes to the cocktail shaker. We like to serve this drink over ice cubes, too, but that's optional.

HOW DO I MAKE THIS?

Add all the ingredients to the cocktail shaker with ice. Shake and strain the drink into the glass, over ice if you like. Garnish with the red chillies and lime wheel.

SPICY & DRY   WARMING/INDULGENT

Marvellous Marmalade Martini

With its zesty orange peel and natural sweetness, marmalade is a great ingredient for a mixed drink, bringing it a depth of flavour in a simple spoonful. This classic cocktail often appears on menus as an option with brunch, but our favourite time to enjoy it is as a post-lunch, pre-dinner balance, where you might be moving from sweeter drinks to something a little bolder.

- ◆ 2 parts vodka
- ◆ 1 part triple sec
- ◆ 1 teaspoon marmalade
- ◆ splash of water

WHICH GLASS?

A V-shaped cocktail glass or coupe.

WHAT ABOUT A GARNISH?

A thin piece of orange peel (optional).

WHAT EQUIPMENT WILL I NEED?

A jigger measure, teaspoon and cocktail shaker and strainer.

DO I ADD ICE?

Add ice cubes to the cocktail shaker, but not to the glass.

HOW DO I MAKE THIS?

Add all the ingredients to the cocktail shaker and 'dry shake' without ice. Then add ice and shake again. Strain the drink into your glass and garnish with orange peel if you like.

SWEET & FRUITY   CELEBRATION/PARTY STARTER

Mocha Martini

The Espresso Martini has become a revelation, with its dark-roasted, malty sweetness, making it a proper party starter. But imagine how much better it might be with a spoonful of chocolate hazelnut spread added to the cocktail shaker! This drink is nutty, chocolaty and utterly moreish.

- 2 parts freshly brewed and cooled espresso coffee
  - 1 part dark rum
  - 1 teaspoon chocolate hazelnut spread

WHICH GLASS?

A V-shaped cocktail glass or coupe.

WHAT ABOUT A GARNISH?

A dusting of drinking chocolate powder.

WHAT EQUIPMENT WILL I NEED?

A jigger measure, teaspoon and cocktail shaker and strainer.

DO I ADD ICE?

Add ice cubes to the cocktail shaker, but not to the glass.

HOW DO I MAKE THIS?

Add all the ingredients to the cocktail shaker and give a quick stir with the teaspoon. Add ice and shake, then strain into your glass. Dust with drinking chocolate powder.

COMPLEX & RICH   CELEBRATION/PARTY STARTER

Blockbuster Passion Fruit Daiquiri

The Passion Fruit Martini is a drink that has taken the world by storm, mostly because passion fruit is bloomin' tasty! Our blockbuster version takes all the great parts of the aforementioned cocktail and pulls them well and truly into the limelight with zingy notes of passion fruit and lively lime flavours.

- ◆ 1 passion fruit
- ◆ 2 parts white rum
- ◆ 1 part freshly squeezed lime juice
- ◆ ½ part simple sugar syrup (see page 24 for homemade)

WHICH GLASS?

A V-shaped cocktail glass or coupe.

WHAT ABOUT A GARNISH?

None needed.

WHAT EQUIPMENT WILL I NEED?

A jigger measure and cocktail shaker and strainer.

DO I ADD ICE?

Add ice cubes to the cocktail shaker, but not to the glass.

HOW DO I MAKE THIS?

Cut the passion fruit in half and scoop out the flesh into the cocktail shaker. Add the rum, lime juice and sugar syrup with ice, then shake and strain into your chosen glass.

SWEET & FRUITY   CHIC/SOPHISTICATED

Olive Oil Gibson

The classic Gibson cocktail is a distinctly savoury twist on a Martini, historically using a small silverskin cocktail onion as a garnish. It has a terrific balance of dry, herbal flavours, but they can be a little too punchy for some, so when you bring in the smooth, rich-but-peppery notes of a quality virgin olive oil for company, things take a completely different turn.

- ◆ **3 parts gin** – a more savoury style of gin works really well here, such as Gin Mare
- ◆ **½ part dry vermouth** – or add another ½ part for a 'wetter' cocktail
- ◆ **extra virgin olive oil,** for drizzling

WHICH GLASS?

A V-shaped cocktail glass or coupe.

WHAT ABOUT A GARNISH?

A small cocktail onion, on a stick if you like, or, if you're a fan, a small gherkin.

WHAT EQUIPMENT WILL I NEED?

A jigger measure, mixing glass, bar spoon and cocktail strainer.

DO I ADD ICE?

Add ice cubes to the mixing glass, but not to the serving glass. Instead, chill the glass in the freezer beforehand (see page 13).

HOW DO I MAKE THIS?

Add the gin and vermouth to the mixing glass with ice and stir with the bar spoon for 15 seconds. Strain into your chilled glass, then carefully drizzle half a dozen drops of extra virgin olive oil on to the surface of the drink. Finally, add the garnish.

SPICY & DRY   CHIC/SOPHISTICATED

St Clement's

Who doesn't love a Cosmopolitan? The pink drink that took the world by storm in neon nightclubs the world over in the late 1990s is a winner. But you might not always have cranberry juice to hand, so if you want a sweeter, fruity kick, then try a St Clement's instead.

◆ 2 parts freshly squeezed orange juice

◆ 1 part vodka

◆ 1 part triple sec

◆ ½ part freshly squeezed lemon juice

WHICH GLASS?

A coupe or V-shaped cocktail glass.

WHAT ABOUT A GARNISH?

None needed.

WHAT EQUIPMENT WILL I NEED?

A jigger measure and cocktail shaker and strainer.

DO I ADD ICE?

Add ice cubes to the cocktail shaker, but not to the glass.

HOW DO I MAKE THIS?

Add all the ingredients to the cocktail shaker with ice and shake, then strain into your chosen glass.

SWEET & FRUITY   CHIC/SOPHISTICATED

The Classic Whiskey Sour

The Whiskey Sour is another classic drink that has stood the test of time, thanks to its incredible versatility: you can bring any whisk(e)y to the party, be it Scotch, American, Canadian, Japanese or Irish, and it still shines. We've settled on using an Irish blended whiskey, as it's perhaps the ultimate all-rounder – sweet, with a hint of malt and a delicious fruity balance.

- 1 medium egg white or 1 part aquafaba
- 2 parts Irish whiskey – Jameson or Bushmills are both excellent choices
- 1 part freshly squeezed lemon juice
- ½ part simple sugar syrup (see page 24 for homemade)
- 6 drops Angostura bitters

WHICH GLASS?

A rocks glass or short tumbler.

WHAT ABOUT A GARNISH?

None needed for this baby!

WHAT EQUIPMENT WILL I NEED?

A jigger measure and cocktail shaker and strainer.

DO I ADD ICE?

Yes, add a few large ice cubes that stay below the rim of the glass and plenty of ice cubes to the cocktail shaker.

HOW DO I MAKE THIS?

Add the large ice cubes to the glass. Then add the egg white or aquafaba to a cocktail shaker and shake without ice for 10 seconds into a foam. Add the whiskey, lemon juice and sugar syrup and half-fill the shaker with ice. Shake for 8–10 seconds and strain into the glass. Carefully place the drops of bitters on top of the foam and use a cocktail stick to create a pattern.

COMPLEX & RICH

WARMING/INDULGENT

Cheat's Brandy Alexander

Almost as much a dessert as a drink, the Brandy Alexander is utterly decadent, rich and full of flavour. The traditional recipe calls for crème de cacao, which brings a chocolaty note to the drink. Our version is much easier. Just reach for a tub of unctuous, smooth chocolate ice cream and moments later you'll find yourself in rich cocktail heaven!

◆ 1 small scoop smooth chocolate ice cream (no bits!)
◆ 1 part French brandy
◆ 2 parts almond milk

WHICH GLASS?

A small wine glass or V-shaped cocktail glass.

WHAT ABOUT A GARNISH?

A grating of nutmeg.

WHAT EQUIPMENT WILL I NEED?

A jigger measure, cocktail shaker and strainer and bar spoon.

DO I ADD ICE?

Add a few ice cubes to the cocktail shaker, but not to the glass.

HOW DO I MAKE THIS?

Add all the ingredients to the cocktail shaker and quickly stir with the bar spoon. Add the ice, shake for a few seconds and then strain into your chosen glass. Grate some nutmeg over the top to finish.

COMPLEX & RICH   WARMING/INDULGENT

Fabulous French 75

Timeless and elegant, the French 75 dates back well over a century and, rather surprisingly, takes its name from a 75mm military field gun! However, as knockout as the drink's flavour may be, there's a wonderful subtlety to it, too, balancing gin, citrus and the sweetness of sugar. It's a cocktail that whenever you make one, it will certainly bring the house down.

- ◆ 1 part gin
- ◆ ½ part freshly squeezed lemon juice
- ◆ ½ part simple sugar syrup (see page 24 for homemade)
- ◆ 4 parts Champagne or other sparkling wine

WHICH GLASS?

A flute.

WHAT ABOUT A GARNISH?

A thin piece or spiral of lemon peel.

WHAT EQUIPMENT WILL I NEED?

A jigger measure and cocktail shaker and strainer.

DO I ADD ICE?

Add ice cubes to the cocktail shaker, but not to the glass.

HOW DO I MAKE THIS?

Add the gin, lemon juice and sugar syrup to the cocktail shaker with ice. Give it a good shake and strain into your flute. Top up with the sparkling wine and garnish with the piece or spiral of lemon peel.

SIMPLE & REFRESHING   CELEBRATION/PARTY STARTER

Wondermint Julep

Among the greatest bourbon-based cocktails is the Mint Julep. This cocktail's simple ingredients are the key to its longevity. It's also wonderfully easy to personalize, too, taking it in any direction you choose: from adding a different variety of mint, such as lemon mint, or a sprig of fresh thyme for something more herbaceous, to a different type of sugar syrup, such as muscovado, for a more malty, toasted flavour, which we've used here.

- ½ part muscovado sugar syrup (see page 24 for homemade)
- 1 dash water
- handful of fresh mint leaves
- 2 parts American whiskey – try a quality bourbon like Maker's Mark or Wild Turkey

WHICH GLASS?

Traditionally served in a chilled metal julep cup, but we have used a metal camping mug. You can really use any short tumbler. Chilling it in the freezer will help.

WHAT ABOUT A GARNISH?

Sprigs of fresh mint and an optional dusting of icing sugar.

WHAT EQUIPMENT WILL I NEED?

A jigger measure, cocktail shaker and strainer and muddler.

DO I ADD ICE?

Yes, add crushed ice to your chilled mug and ice cubes to the cocktail shaker.

HOW DO I MAKE THIS?

First, add the crushed ice to your chilled mug. Then add the sugar syrup and water to the cocktail shaker followed by the mint leaves and crush them down slightly with the muddler. Next, add the whiskey and some ice cubes and give it a good shake for 8 seconds. Strain into the mug and garnish with sprigs of mint. Some people like to add a dusting of icing sugar for additional effect. Up to you. We think you're sweet enough!

SIMPLE & REFRESHING   EASY-GOING/EVERYDAY

Side Hustle

The Sidecar is a luscious, punchy classic cocktail that combines the bittersweet orange tones of triple sec with the vibrant notes of citrus and rich, deep flavours from aged French brandy. This refreshing version lengthens the drink with lemonade and serves it over ice. Less of the freewheeling feeling of the original, more of a longer, enjoyable, comfortable journey.

- 2 parts French brandy
- 1 part triple sec
- ½ part freshly squeezed lemon juice
- 4 parts lemonade

WHICH GLASS?

A highball or other tall glass.

WHAT ABOUT A GARNISH?

A thin piece of lemon peel.

WHAT EQUIPMENT WILL I NEED?

A jigger measure, cocktail shaker and strainer and bar spoon.

DO I ADD ICE?

Yes, add ice cubes to the glass and to the cocktail shaker.

HOW DO I MAKE THIS?

First, add ice to your glass. Then add all the ingredients except the lemonade to the cocktail shaker with ice and shake. Strain into the glass and top up with the lemonade. Give the drink a gentle stir with the bar spoon, then garnish with the lemon peel.

SIMPLE & REFRESHING   CELEBRATION/PARTY STARTER

Ramblin' Bramble

This novel take on the classic Bramble cheats a little in that we're using blackcurrant cordial and pink gin instead of traditional crème de mûre and sugar syrup. It's deliciously fruity, refreshing and fit to revivify and restore after a weekend's ramble through the countryside, or your local park.

- ◆ 2 parts pink gin
- ◆ 1 part freshly squeezed lemon juice
- ◆ 1 part blackcurrant cordial

WHICH GLASS?

A rocks glass or short tumbler.

WHAT ABOUT A GARNISH?

A fresh lemon wheel and a fresh blackberry.

WHAT EQUIPMENT WILL I NEED?

A jigger measure, cocktail shaker and strainer and bar spoon.

DO I ADD ICE?

Yes, add crushed ice to the glass and ice cubes to the cocktail shaker.

HOW DO I MAKE THIS?

First, add the crushed ice to your glass. Then add the pink gin and lemon juice to the cocktail shaker, half-fill with ice cubes and shake for 10 seconds. Strain into the glass and drizzle over the blackcurrant cordial. Give a quick stir with the bar spoon and garnish with the lemon wheel and blackberry.

SWEET & FRUITY   EASY-GOING/EVERYDAY

Buzzin' Bee's Knees

A really great classic that brings together sweet honey, zesty lemon and a herbaceous kick of gin, the Bee's Knees is a drink that will please all palates and is sure to get the party buzzing! We have added orange juice to the mix, too, to give this an extra level of fruitiness.

- ◆ 2 parts gin
- ◆ 1 part freshly squeezed lemon juice
- ◆ 1 part freshly squeezed orange juice
- ◆ ½ part clear honey, first loosened with a little warm water

WHICH GLASS?

A coupe or V-shaped cocktail glass.

WHAT ABOUT A GARNISH?

None needed.

WHAT EQUIPMENT WILL I NEED?

A jigger measure and cocktail shaker and strainer.

DO I ADD ICE?

Add ice cubes to the cocktail shaker, but not to the glass.

HOW DO I MAKE THIS?

Add all the ingredients to the cocktail shaker and 'dry shake' without ice. Then add ice and shake again. Strain into your chosen glass.

COMPLEX & RICH   CHIC/SOPHISTICATED

The Big Apple

A sweeter, fruitier twist on a Whiskey Sour that dials up the earthy, vanilla-led fruitiness with an American bourbon. Apple and bourbon really are a match made in heaven, and adding a measure of fresh apple juice brings out some of the drier, complex flavours in the whiskey while giving a lovely refreshing sweetness.

- 1 medium egg white or 1 part aquafaba
- 2 parts bourbon
- 2 parts clear apple juice
- 1 part freshly squeezed lime juice
- ½ part simple sugar syrup (see page 24 for homemade)

WHICH GLASS?

A coupe, please!

WHAT ABOUT A GARNISH?

A dusting of ground cinnamon.

WHAT EQUIPMENT WILL I NEED?

A jigger measure and cocktail shaker and strainer.

DO I ADD ICE?

Add ice cubes to the cocktail shaker, but not to the glass.

HOW DO I MAKE THIS?

Add the egg white or aquafaba to the cocktail shaker and 'dry shake' without ice for about 10 seconds into a foam. Then add the remaining ingredients with ice and shake for another 10 seconds. Strain into the glass. Hold a card above the drink and dust with cinnamon for a sharp-edged finish.

SWEET & FRUITY   WARMING/INDULGENT

Fizzy Lizzy

This lovely long drink brings together the depth of aged brandy with sweet and slightly spicy notes from sweet vermouth and a little raspberry jam for an additional level of fruitiness. Once the three are combined, they become greater than the sum of their parts!

- ◆ 2 parts sweet vermouth
- ◆ 1 part French brandy
- ◆ 1 teaspoon seedless raspberry jam
- ◆ 1 dash water
- ◆ 4 parts sparkling water

WHICH GLASS?

A tall highball glass.

WHAT ABOUT A GARNISH?

Fresh raspberries work a treat.

WHAT EQUIPMENT WILL I NEED?

A jigger measure, teaspoon, cocktail shaker and strainer and bar spoon.

DO I ADD ICE?

Yes, add ice cubes to the glass and to the cocktail shaker.

HOW DO I MAKE THIS?

First, fill your glass with ice. Then add the sweet vermouth, brandy and jam to the cocktail shaker with ice and the water. Shake hard for a few seconds. Pour into the glass and top up with the sparkling water. Stir gently with the bar spoon to mix and then garnish with the fresh raspberries.

SWEET & FRUITY   EASY-GOING/EVERYDAY

Cincuenta/ Cincuenta

Tequila and beer are wonderful bedfellows, and the slightly sour-yet-fruity notes of a hopped IPA mirror the grapefruit notes in a Paloma, one of the most refreshing tequila drinks out there (see page 30). This drink builds on the earthy notes of tequila with a zesty IPA, a touch of citrus and some sweetness from triple sec.

- ◆ 2 parts silver (*blanco*) tequila
- ◆ 1 part freshly squeezed lemon juice
- ◆ 1 part triple sec
- ◆ 4 parts well-chilled fruity IPA

WHICH GLASS?

A tall highball glass.

WHAT ABOUT A GARNISH?

A fresh grapefruit slice (optional).

WHAT EQUIPMENT WILL I NEED?

A jigger measure and bar spoon.

DO I ADD ICE?

Yes, fill the glass to the top with ice cubes.

HOW DO I MAKE THIS?

Fill your glass with ice, then add all the ingredients, with the IPA going in last. Give the drink a gentle stir with the bar spoon to mix, then garnish with a grapefruit slice if you like.

SPICY & DRY   EASY-GOING/EVERYDAY

Sparkling Speakeasy Spice

This drink is based on The Chicago Fizz, a lost classic at the height of its powers just before Prohibition hit America, which brings together rum, port and lemon juice. Our version uses spiced rum, sweet vermouth, sugar syrup, egg white (or aquafaba) and orange juice. Served long over ice and lengthened with sparkling water, it is a deviously rich, silky and flavoursome fizzy drink.

- ◆ 2 parts spiced rum
- ◆ 1 part sweet vermouth – or use ruby port instead
- ◆ 1 part freshly squeezed orange juice
- ◆ ½ part simple sugar syrup (see page 24 for homemade)
- ◆ 1 medium egg white or 1 part aquafaba
- ◆ 2 parts sparkling water

WHICH GLASS?

A tall highball glass.

WHAT ABOUT A GARNISH?

None needed.

WHAT EQUIPMENT WILL I NEED?

A jigger measure and cocktail shaker and strainer.

DO I ADD ICE?

Yes, add ice cubes to the glass and to the cocktail shaker.

HOW DO I MAKE THIS?

First, add plenty of ice to your glass. Them add all the ingredients except the sparkling water to the cocktail shaker and, erm, shake! Strain into the glass and slowly top up with the sparkling water.

COMPLEX & RICH   WARMING/INDULGENT

Cucumber Cooler

The ultimate in refreshment, this is a drink for when the sun is shining, the land is dry and your thirst is high! The combination of crisp vodka, cool cucumber, zesty lime juice and sweetness, lengthened with vibrant sparkling water, is an oasis for the palate. It can easily be batched in a pitcher for big groups, too.

- ¼ cucumber, cut into small cubes
- 1 part freshly squeezed lime juice
- 1 part simple sugar syrup (see page 24 for homemade)
- 2 parts vodka
- 4 parts sparkling water

WHICH GLASS?

A highball glass.

WHAT ABOUT A GARNISH?

A fresh cucumber ribbon (see page 23).

WHAT EQUIPMENT WILL I NEED?

A jigger measure, cocktail shaker and strainer and muddler.

DO I ADD ICE?

Yes, add ice cubes to the glass and to the cocktail shaker.

HOW DO I MAKE THIS?

First, fill your glass with ice. Then add the cucumber cubes to the cocktail shaker and crush down with the muddler. Add the lime juice, sugar syrup and vodka and shake. Strain into the glass and top up with the sparkling water. Garnish with the cucumber ribbon.

SIMPLE & REFRESHING   CELEBRATION/PARTY STARTER   GOOD FOR BATCHING

Brite-Side

If you're looking to explore the world of low-ABV or non-alcoholic cocktails, then using different teas as the base is a great place to start. From smoky lapsang souchong to green tea and even an everyday black tea brew, tea contributes lots of dry, tannic structure to a drink. The Brite-Side brings together the subtle floral notes of Earl Grey, a little spice from Angostura bitters and the dry fruitiness of cloudy apple juice.

- ◆ 2 parts freshly brewed and cooled Earl Grey tea (no milk!)
- ◆ 2 parts cloudy apple juice
- ◆ ½ part freshly squeezed lemon juice
- ◆ 2 dashes Angostura bitters

WHICH GLASS?

A small coupe.

WHAT ABOUT A GARNISH?

A thin piece of lemon peel, with a slit cut down the middle.

WHAT EQUIPMENT WILL I NEED?

A jigger measure and cocktail shaker and strainer.

DO I ADD ICE?

Add ice cubes to the cocktail shaker, but not to the glass.

HOW DO I MAKE THIS?

Add all the ingredients to the cocktail shaker and half-fill with ice. Shake vigorously for 10 seconds, then strain into the glass. Squeeze the lemon peel over the top of the drink to express the oils (see page 22) and then place on the rim to garnish.

SPICY & DRY   EASY-GOING/EVERYDAY

Magnificent Mixes

Special drinks for those more decadent drinking occasions that require a little more preparation or an unusual ingredient here and there

Heart Peat

This one is a play on another classic called the Blood & Sand, a drink that takes its name from a 1922 Rudolph Valentino movie of the same name. The star performer in this cinematic cocktail is a feisty, powerful, sultry, smoky Scotch whisky, which brings character, a touch of dryness and plenty of charisma.

- ◆ 1 part smoky whisky – we recommend Laphroaig
- ◆ 1 part freshly squeezed blood orange juice
- ◆ 1 part sweet vermouth
- ◆ ½ part cherry brandy – we recommend Heering Cherry Liqueur

WHICH GLASS?

A coupe, or vintage goblet if you can find one!

WHAT ABOUT A GARNISH?

A fresh mint leaf.

WHAT EQUIPMENT WILL I NEED?

A jigger measure and cocktail shaker and strainer.

DO I ADD ICE?

Add ice cubes to the cocktail shaker, but not to the glass. Instead, chill your glass beforehand for a frosted look (see page 13).

HOW DO I MAKE THIS?

Add all the ingredients to the cocktail shaker, half-fill with ice and shake for 10 seconds. Strain into your glass and place the mint leaf on the surface of the drink to garnish.

COMPLEX & RICH

CHIC/SOPHISTICATED

Banana Bread Daiquiri

The lockdown may have turned us into would-be baking stars, but is it possible to enjoy the flavours of all that wonderfully stodgy comfort food without piling on too many pounds? Of course it is! We've combined two of our favourite lockdown treats in one sitting to create a banana-bread-infused dark rum, which forms the base for this deliciously moreish, unctuous Daiquiri.

- ◆ 2½ parts banana-bread-infused dark rum (see below)
- ◆ ½ part freshly squeezed lime juice
- ◆ ½ part triple sec
- ◆ ½ part simple sugar syrup or spiced sugar syrup (see pages 24 and 25), optional

WHICH GLASS?

A coupe.

WHAT ABOUT A GARNISH?

None needed, but a slice of freshly baked homemade banana bread is the perfect accompaniment!

WHAT EQUIPMENT WILL I NEED?

A measuring jug, tea strainer, jigger measure, cocktail shaker and strainer.

DO I ADD ICE?

Add ice cubes to the cocktail shaker, but not to the glass.

HOW DO I MAKE THIS?

Add all the ingredients to the cocktail shaker, half-fill with ice and shake for 8–10 seconds. Strain into your glass.

BANANA-BREAD-INFUSED RUM

Put 200ml (7fl oz) of dark rum and a large slice of banana bread into a jar. Seal and steep for at least 24 hours. Fine strain when ready. Makes 2–3 drinks.

COMPLEX & RICH   WARMING/INDULGENT   GOOD FOR BATCHING

Elderflower Gimlet

The classic Gimlet highlights all the lovely zesty, fruity sharpness of lime and gin working in harmony together. However, if you fancy mixing up this classic into a real summer smash, with a few simple tweaks it can become a floral delight, too.

- ◆ 2 parts London Dry gin
- ◆ 1 part freshly squeezed lemon juice
- ◆ 2 dashes orange Angostura bitters
- ◆ ½ part elderflower cordial
- ◆ 1 medium egg white or 1 part aquafaba

WHICH GLASS?

An elegant coupe.

WHAT ABOUT A GARNISH?

A thin piece of lemon peel and, when in season, a small head of elderflower blossom (stalk removed).

WHAT EQUIPMENT WILL I NEED?

A jigger measure and cocktail shaker and strainer.

DO I ADD ICE?

Add ice cubes to the cocktail shaker, but not to the glass.

HOW DO I MAKE THIS?

Add the egg white or aquafaba to the shaker and 'dry shake' without ice for about 10 seconds into a foam. Then add the remaining ingredients, half-fill the shaker with ice and shake for another 8–10 seconds. Strain into the glass. Squeeze the lemon peel over the top of the drink to express the oils (see page 22) and add to the glass to garnish. Garnish with the elderflower as well, when available.

SWEET & FRUITY   CHIC/SOPHISTICATED

Best Ever Piña Colada

With its roots in Puerto Rico, the Piña Colada has become famous the world over. Hopefully you'll love our version, too, which builds on the classic recipe but adds sweetness in the form of canned pineapple. This recipe makes enough to serve two.

- ◆ **225g (8oz) canned pineapple rings in syrup**
- ◆ **1 part white rum**
- ◆ **1 part coconut cream**
- ◆ **½ part freshly squeezed lime juice**

WHICH GLASS?

Two Hurricane glasses or tall highball glasses.

WHAT ABOUT A GARNISH?

Two small pineapple wedges, canned or fresh.

WHAT EQUIPMENT WILL I NEED?

A jigger measure and blender.

DO I ADD ICE?

Add ice cubes to the blender, but not to the glasses.

HOW DO I MAKE THIS?

Add the pineapple and syrup from the can to the blender with the other ingredients and a cupful of ice cubes, then blitz until smooth. Pour into your chosen glasses and garnish each with a pineapple wedge.

SWEET & FRUITY   **EASY-GOING/EVERYDAY**   **GOOD FOR BATCHING**

King of Roses

If one cocktail deserves to become a classic, it's this, originally created by a good friend of ours, Mr Will Foster, in his now legendary but sadly long-since closed bar Casita in London. A devilishly complex blend of flavours from bourbon, The King's Ginger (a warming, sweet ginger liqueur first created for King Edward VII) and fresh citrus juices, we'll happily take up the mantle of trying to keep its memory alive. If you prefer a sweeter version, add a dash of spiced sugar syrup (see page 25) to the shaker.

- ◆ **2 parts bourbon** – the original calls for Four Roses, but any quality bourbon works well
- ◆ **1 part The King's Ginger**
- ◆ **2 parts freshly squeezed orange juice**
- ◆ **1 part freshly squeezed lemon juice**

WHICH GLASS?

A coupe.

WHAT ABOUT A GARNISH?

None needed.

WHAT EQUIPMENT WILL I NEED?

A jigger measure, cocktail shaker and strainer and tea strainer.

DO I ADD ICE?

Add ice cubes to the cocktail shaker, but not to the glass.

HOW DO I MAKE THIS?

Add all the ingredients to the cocktail shaker, half-fill with ice and shake for 10 seconds. Fine strain through the tea strainer into the glass.

SWEET & FRUITY

WARMING/INDULGENT

El Presidente

This relatively reserved rum cocktail feels like it deserves much more attention at the top table of true classics, which it very much is! Supposedly created in Cuba back in the 1910s, it traditionally brings together lighter golden rum (not as heavy or oak-aged as traditional dark rum), sweet and dry vermouths, curaçao and grenadine (a ruby-red, pomegranate-based syrup), stirred together until perfectly balanced.

- ◆ 1 part white rum
- ◆ 1 part dark rum
- ◆ 1 part sweet vermouth
- ◆ ½ part dry vermouth
- ◆ ½ part curaçao
- ◆ 2 dashes grenadine syrup
- ◆ 1 dash chocolate bitters (optional)

WHICH GLASS?

A coupe.

WHAT ABOUT A GARNISH?

A thin piece of orange peel.

WHAT EQUIPMENT WILL I NEED?

A jigger measure, mixing glass, bar spoon and cocktail strainer.

DO I ADD ICE?

Add ice cubes to the mixing glass, but not to the serving glass. Instead, chill the glass down beforehand (see page 13).

HOW DO I MAKE THIS?

Add all the ingredients to the mixing glass, including the chocolate bitters if you want some additional depth. Fill with ice and gently stir with the bar spoon for 15–20 seconds. Strain into your chilled coupe. Squeeze the orange peel over the top of the drink to express the oils (see page 22) and drop into the glass to garnish.

SPICY & DRY   CHIC/SOPHISTICATED

New Orleans Legend

Variations of this drink, often called a Sazerac, have been around since the middle of the 19th century. It majors on an unlikely pairing of two spirit heroes, French brandy and American whiskey, combined with a touch of the highly distinctive absinthe. On paper, it may sound like an absolute firecracker waiting to explode, but in practice, the blend of sweet, savoury and herbal flavours is hard to beat.

- ◆ 1 part bourbon or other American whiskey
- ◆ 1 part Cognac or other French brandy
- ◆ ½ part simple sugar syrup (see page 24 for homemade)
- ◆ 2 dashes Peychaud's bitters
- ◆ 1 dash absinthe

WHICH GLASS?

A rocks glass or short tumbler.

WHAT ABOUT A GARNISH?

A thin piece of lemon peel.

WHAT EQUIPMENT WILL I NEED?

A jigger measure, mixing glass, bar spoon and cocktail strainer.

DO I ADD ICE?

Add ice cubes to the mixing glass, but not to the glass. Instead, chill the glass in the freezer beforehand (see page 13).

HOW DO I MAKE THIS?

Add all the ingredients except the absinthe to the mixing glass with ice and stir with the bar spoon for 15 seconds. Add the absinthe to your chilled glass and swirl until the inside is coated. Strain the drink into the glass. Squeeze the lemon peel over the top of the drink to express the oils (see page 22) and add to garnish.

SPICY & DRY   CHIC/SOPHISTICATED

The 'Vamos' Gin Fizz

The Ramos Gin Fizz, a creamy gin-based drink with a light, frothy, almost soufflé-like head, is an undisputed classic. We've come up with a little life hack to make an excellent Ramos-style drink that won't take five minutes to make and leave your arms numb from a full-on shaker workout! #sorrynotsorry.

- ◆ 2 parts London Dry gin
- ◆ 1 large scoop lemon sorbet
- ◆ 1 medium egg white or 1 part aquafaba
- ◆ 1 part almond milk
- ◆ 2 dashes orange Angostura bitters
- ◆ ½ part freshly squeezed lime juice
- ◆ 5 parts chilled sparkling water

WHICH GLASS?

A tall, thin highball glass.

WHAT ABOUT A GARNISH?

A thin orange wedge, with a small cut in to fix the orange to the side of the glass.

WHAT EQUIPMENT WILL I NEED?

A jigger measure, a cocktail shaker and strainer and bar spoon.

DO I ADD ICE?

None needed, but for best results, chill the glass in the freezer beforehand (see page 13).

HOW DO I MAKE THIS?

Add all the ingredients except the sparkling water to the cocktail shaker and shake vigorously for 10–15 seconds. Strain into your chilled glass and top up with the sparkling water to the brim. Then slowly pour a little more sparkling water down the shaft of the bar spoon until the frothy head rises up impressively. Place the orange wedge on the rim to garnish.

SWEET & FRUITY   CHIC/SOPHISTICATED

Mexican Mole Old-Fashioned

The Old-Fashioned is arguably one of THE classic cocktails that truly started the world's love affair with the mixed drink. This twist on the original brings together the rounded flavour of aged tequila, rich chocolate bitters and a hint of fruity cherry notes for a Mexican mole-inspired drink.

- ◆ 2 parts *añejo* (aged) tequila
- ◆ ¼ part cherry liqueur
- ◆ ½ part muscovado sugar syrup (see page 24 for homemade)
- ◆ 2 dashes chocolate bitters

WHICH GLASS?

A rocks glass or short tumbler.

WHAT ABOUT A GARNISH?

A small cocktail cherry.

WHAT EQUIPMENT WILL I NEED?

A jigger measure, mixing glass, bar spoon and cocktail strainer.

DO I ADD ICE?

Yes, add a large ice block to the serving glass and ice cubes to the mixing glass.

HOW DO I MAKE THIS?

First, add the ice block to your serving glass. Then add all the ingredients to the mixing glass with ice cubes and stir with the bar spoon for 15–20 seconds. Strain into the glass and garnish with the cocktail cherry.

COMPLEX & RICH   WARMING/INDULGENT

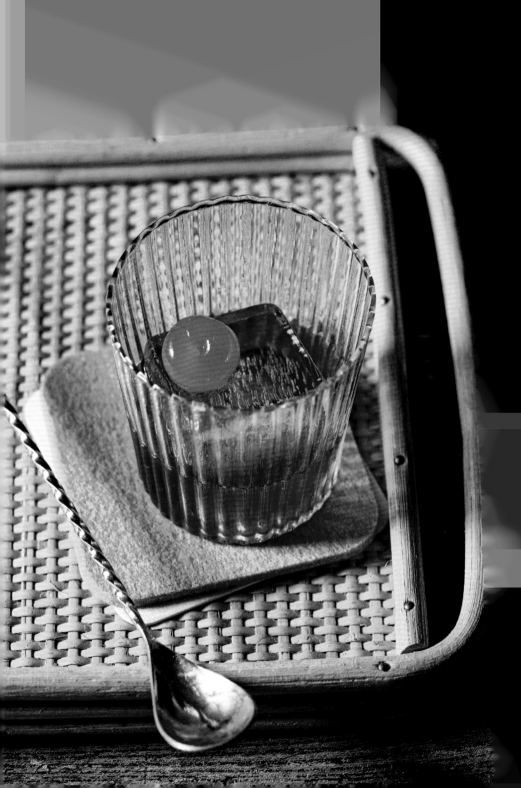

Nan's Sherry Trifle

As it's a seasonal drink, you're probably only going to see advocaat, or eggnog, the custard-like, egg-based liqueur, go on sale in December for making Snowballs. We've used that traditional classic cocktail here as a template to create a liquid take on another festive treat, the sherry trifle, which brings back so many happy and tasty memories!

- 3 parts advocaat – Warninks is the classic – or eggnog
- 1 part amontillado or oloroso sherry
- ½ part cherry liqueur
- 2 dashes chocolate bitters
- 4–5 parts ginger ale

WHICH GLASS?

A large wine glass or Hurricane glass.

WHAT ABOUT A GARNISH?

A dusting of grated nutmeg, a cocktail cherry on a cocktail stick and some optional flaked almonds.

WHAT EQUIPMENT WILL I NEED?

A jigger measure and bar spoon.

DO I ADD ICE?

Yes, some large ice cubes are perfect.

HOW DO I MAKE THIS?

Add all the ingredients except the ginger ale to your glass and stir with the bar spoon for a few seconds to mix together. Add the ice and top up slowly with the ginger ale, giving a final stir to bring a creamy, frothy head to the drink. Grate some nutmeg on the top, add the cherry on its cocktail stick and sprinkle the top of the drink with flaked almonds to garnish, if you like.

COMPLEX & RICH

WARMING/INDULGENT

CDMX aka Mexico City

This twist on a classic Manhattan takes it to a whole new level, or at least a whole new country, by using earthy, smoky mezcal with sweet vermouth and orange bitters for what we have called a CDMX or Mexico City, in homage to the original New Yorker name.

- ◆ 2 parts mezcal
- ◆ 1 part sweet vermouth
- ◆ 3 dashes orange Angostura bitters
- ◆ 1 teaspoon water

WHICH GLASS?

A coupe.

WHAT ABOUT A GARNISH?

A thin piece of orange peel.

WHAT EQUIPMENT WILL I NEED?

A jigger measure, teaspoon, cocktail shaker and strainer and tea strainer.

DO I ADD ICE?

Add ice cubes to the cocktail shaker, but not to the glass. Instead, chill the glass in the freezer beforehand (see page 13).

HOW DO I MAKE THIS?

Add all the ingredients to the cocktail shaker with ice, then give it a good shake for 8–10 seconds. Fine strain through the tea strainer into the chilled glass and garnish with the orange peel.

COMPLEX & RICH   CHIC/SOPHISTICATED

Sensational Sherbet Fizz

A fruity variety of IPA carries some big flavours that are fantastic on their own, but it can also be mixed with other ingredients to enhance its zingy, citrusy nature. In this sensational tongue-tingler, the zesty IPA works with sweet cherry notes and bitter Campari for a drink that is surprisingly refreshing yet dry.

- 1 part cherry brandy
- ½ part Campari
- 3 dashes orange Angostura bitters
- 4 parts well-chilled fruity IPA

WHICH GLASS?

A flute.

WHAT ABOUT A GARNISH?

None needed.

WHAT EQUIPMENT WILL I NEED?

A jigger measure and bar spoon.

DO I ADD ICE?

None needed, but ensure the IPA is ice-cold from the refrigerator.

HOW DO I MAKE THIS?

Add the cherry brandy, Campari and bitters to the flute and give the ingredients a quick stir with the bar spoon to mix. Slowly add the IPA, then gently lift and give a final stir with the spoon.

SIMPLE & REFRESHING

EASY-GOING/EVERYDAY

Millionaire's Black Velvet

The Black Velvet is a drink that traditionally brings together the best examples of two country's flagship drinks: Irish stout and French Champagne. Our take on the original gives it a fruity richness (hence the addition of 'Millionaire' to its title!) and tastes like you're drinking the classic combo with a slice of Black Forest gateau on the side.

- ◆ 1 part Chambord
- ◆ 3 parts chilled stout, such as Guinness
- ◆ 3 parts chilled sparkling wine

WHICH GLASS?

A wine glass.

WHAT ABOUT A GARNISH?

A fresh cherry.

WHAT EQUIPMENT WILL I NEED?

A jigger measure and bar spoon.

DO I ADD ICE?

None needed, but ensure the stout and sparkling wine are cold from the refrigerator.

HOW DO I MAKE THIS?

Add the Chambord to your glass and then slowly add the stout. Next, carefully pour in the sparkling wine and finally slowly lift and mix the ingredients with the bar spoon a couple of times. Garnish with the cherry. Once you've made this a few times, you can dispense with measuring the stout and sparkling wine, and simply pour both into the glass by eye and adjust to your own taste.

COMPLEX & RICH

WARMING/INDULGENT

White Port Cobbler

When it comes to port, you're probably familiar with the ruby variety, which we feature in a couple of drinks in this book (see pages 36 and 106), but are you on tasting terms with the fresh, bright and aromatic white variety? If not, time to grab a bottle of Portugal's 'best-kept secret' from the supermarket! This simple yet balanced Cobbler – a style of cocktail from the early 19th century – is perfect for summer get-togethers.

- ◆ 3 parts white port
- ◆ 1 part freshly squeezed orange juice (or blood orange juice)
- ◆ 1 part pineapple juice
- ◆ ½ part freshly squeezed lemon juice
- ◆ 4 parts Prosecco or other sparkling wine

WHICH GLASS?

A large wine glass or copa.

WHAT ABOUT A GARNISH?

A fresh orange slice.

WHAT EQUIPMENT WILL I NEED?

A jigger measure and bar spoon.

DO I ADD ICE?

Yes, add plenty of crushed ice to the glass.

HOW DO I MAKE THIS?

First, add some crushed ice to your glass. Then pour over all the ingredients except the sparkling wine and stir, lifting the flavours together a little with the bar spoon. Add a little more crushed ice and top up with the sparkling wine. Give a final stir and garnish with the orange slice.

SWEET & FRUITY   CELEBRATION/PARTY STARTER

Black Forest Smash

Black cherry and bourbon is a powerful combo of bold, ripe fruit and delicious, silky vanilla flavours. Throw in a little sweet nuttiness from the black walnut bitters – a versatile variety of bitters that you can also use for enhancing cocktails like the Old-Fashioned – and ginger ale, and you have an awesome feel-good hit for the summer!

- 3 fresh cherries, pitted and sliced
- 1 teaspoon black cherry jam
- 2 parts bourbon
- 2 dashes black walnut bitters
- 5 parts ginger ale

WHICH GLASS?

A tall highball glass.

WHAT ABOUT A GARNISH?

A whole fresh cherry and a cinnamon stick.

WHAT EQUIPMENT WILL I NEED?

A jigger measure, teaspoon, muddler and bar spoon.

DO I ADD ICE?

Yes, add plenty of good-sized ice cubes.

HOW DO I MAKE THIS?

Add the cherries with the jam and half the bourbon to your glass and crush down slightly with the muddler until combined. Then add the other half of the bourbon and the bitters. Fill the glass with ice and top up with the ginger ale. Stir a few times with the bar spoon, then garnish with the cherry and cinnamon stick.

SWEET & FRUITY   EASY-GOING/EVERYDAY

Bastille Day

Calvados is one of our all-time favourite brandies, thanks to its delicious, tangy, cider-like flavours and buttery-rich fruitiness. This drink is refreshing, but also bold and complex, and is the perfect accompaniment to a yummy French dessert like Tarte Tatin. *Santé, mes bon amis!*

- ◆ 1 part Calvados – we recommend Père Magloire VSOP
- ◆ ½ part dark rum
- ◆ ½ part clear honey, first loosened with a little warm water
- ◆ 2 dashes chocolate bitters
- ◆ 4 parts sparkling wine – we recommend Champagne or French Crémant

WHICH GLASS?

A large wine glass.

WHAT ABOUT A GARNISH?

A few fresh green apple slices – see page 23 for how to create an apple fan!

WHAT EQUIPMENT WILL I NEED?

A jigger measure and bar spoon.

DO I ADD ICE?

Yes, add plenty of crushed ice.

HOW DO I MAKE THIS?

Add all the ingredients except the sparkling wine to your glass and mix together with the bar spoon until well combined. Add the crushed ice and top up with the sparkling wine. Lift the flavours through the glass with the spoon and garnish with the apple slices.

SIMPLE & REFRESHING   CELEBRATION/PARTY STARTER

No Thyme To Dine

Mezcal is a Mexican spirit closely associated with tequila, both produced using the agave plant, with a growing reputation for being full of flavour and adding a smoky, earthy note to drinks. This dry-yet-refreshing example combines mezcal, dry vermouth and sparkling water, served long over ice with a garnish of fresh thyme for the perfect pre-dinner drink. Or just skip dinner and move on to more cocktails...

- ◆ 1 part mezcal – try Del Maguey Vida
- ◆ 2 parts dry vermouth
- ◆ 4–5 parts sparkling water

WHICH GLASS?

A tall highball glass

WHAT ABOUT A GARNISH?

A sprig of fresh thyme.

WHAT EQUIPMENT WILL I NEED?

A jigger measure and bar spoon.

DO I ADD ICE?

Yes, add plenty of ice cubes.

HOW DO I MAKE THIS?

Fill your glass with ice, then pour over the mezcal and vermouth. Stir for a few seconds with the bar spoon, then add the sparkling water and stir again. Garnish with the sprig of thyme.

SPICY & DRY

EASY-GOING/EVERYDAY

Ginger Fairy

Absinthe, often called 'the green fairy' thanks to its vivid colour and chequered history (something about drinking too much and seeing fairies, but we won't go into that…), is arguably one of the most potent spirits, but also one of the most flavoursome when brought together with other ingredients, as in the New Orleans Legend (see page 126). Here, it's given star billing in this spicy, herbaceous-yet-sweet, warming and refreshing take on a classic Absinthe Frappé.

- ◆ 1 part absinthe – we recommend La Fée Parisienne, which is available in a 20cl bottle
- ◆ 1 part chilled water
- ◆ ½ part The King's Ginger
- ◆ ½ part simple sugar syrup (see page 24 for homemade)

WHICH GLASS?

A rocks glass or short tumbler, or a fancy wine glass – and a paper straw!

WHAT ABOUT A GARNISH?

A sprig of fresh mint (lemon mint is a wonderful option).

WHAT EQUIPMENT WILL I NEED?

A jigger measure, cocktail shaker and strainer and bar spoon.

DO I ADD ICE?

Yes, add plenty of crushed ice to the glass and ice cubes to the cocktail shaker.

HOW DO I MAKE THIS?

First, fill your chosen glass with crushed ice. Then add all the ingredients to the cocktail shaker, half-fill with ice cubes and shake for 10 seconds. Strain into the glass and stir a few times with the bar spoon. Gently slap the sprig of mint between your palms to release the fragrance and use to garnish the drink, then add the straw.

SPICY & DRY   **WARMING/INDULGENT**

Sage Martini

The simplicity of the Martini has led to its hugely enduring popularity over the last century and there are an extraordinary number of twists and turns the drink can take: from bone dry, to wet to downright dirty! This one is altogether more aromatic and herbaceous, thanks to the white port and the bright, zingy aroma of sage.

- ◆ 2 parts vodka
- ◆ 2 parts white port – for a sweeter version, try Graham's Blend No. 5, or for a drier one, Taylor's Chip Dry, in which case leave out the dry vermouth
- ◆ ½ part dry vermouth
- ◆ 6 fresh sage leaves

WHICH GLASS?

A small coupe.

WHAT ABOUT A GARNISH?

An extra fresh sage leaf.

WHAT EQUIPMENT WILL I NEED?

A jigger measure, cocktail shaker and strainer and tea strainer.

DO I ADD ICE?

Add ice cubes to the cocktail shaker, but not to the glass.

HOW DO I MAKE THIS?

Add the vodka, port and vermouth, if using, to the cocktail shaker. Give the sage leaves a quick slap between your palms to open up their aroma and add to the shaker. Half-fill with ice and shake for 10 seconds. Fine strain through the tea strainer into the glass. Gently slap the extra sage leaf and use to garnish the drink.

SPICY & DRY

CHIC/SOPHISTICATED

Raspberry Shrub

Another great alcohol-free alternative to explore in your cocktails are sweet and fruit vinegars such as balsamic vinegar. When balanced correctly, they give a crisp, spirit-like feel to a cocktail, which works exceptionally well when paired with fresh fruit purée, herbs and bitters and then lengthened with a mixer.

- 1½ parts raspberry purée (see page 24) – or use a shop-bought raspberry smoothie
- ½ part balsamic vinegar
- ½ part freshly squeezed lime juice
- 3 dashes chocolate or black walnut bitters
- 4 parts tonic water

WHICH GLASS?

A flute.

WHAT ABOUT A GARNISH?

A fresh basil leaf.

WHAT EQUIPMENT WILL I NEED?

A jigger measure, cocktail shaker and strainer and bar spoon.

DO I ADD ICE?

Yes, add ice cubes to the cocktail shaker and to the glass.

HOW DO I MAKE THIS?

Add all the ingredients except the tonic water to the cocktail shaker. Half-fill with ice and shake for 5–8 seconds. Strain into the flute, add a few ice cubes and top up with the tonic water, stirring gently with the bar spoon. Garnish with the basil leaf.

SIMPLE & REFRESHING   CELEBRATION/PARTY STARTER   GOOD FOR BATCHING

UK to US Glossary

aniseed/anise

baking tray/baking sheet

car boot sale/yard sale

caster sugar/superfine sugar

charity shop/thrift store

chickpeas/garbanzo beans

chopping board/cutting board

clingfilm/plastic wrap

cocktail stick/toothpick

demerara sugar/light brown raw sugar or turbinado sugar

egg, UK medium /egg, US large

flaked almonds/slivered almonds

forefinger/index finger

gherkin/pickle

icing sugar/confectioner's sugar

jug/pitcher

Kilner jar/Mason jar

kitchen paper/paper towels

lemonade/lemon-flavoured soda (such as 7UP or Sprite)

light muscovado sugar/light brown sugar

nonstick baking paper/ parchment paper

shop-bought/store-bought

sieve/strainer

silverskin onion/pearl onion

soda water/club soda

storecupboard/pantry

tea towel/dish towel

vanilla pod/vanilla bean

Acknowledgements

We'd like to give our special thanks to the following awesome friends, loved ones and colleagues who inspired this book and a few of the recipes, for which we are eternally grateful. Next time we meet at the bar, the drinks are on us!

Denise Bates, Jonathan Christie, Pauline Bache and the wonderful team at Octopus Publishing for continuing to believe in us – we can't thank you enough.

Our awesome agent Martine Carter, Tim Lovejoy, Simon Rimmer, Charlie Critchfield, Grainne Hallinan and Kate Fitch at Remarkable TV, Dorothy and all at ZS Verlag Publishing, Vinny Whiteman, Sarah Birks, Missy Flynn, Viviana Garcia and Rose Mordaunt for making the book look fantastic, Will Foster for the King of Roses recipe (see page 122), Michael Vachon for his incredible olive oil (see page 82), Millie Milliken aka the Martini Queen,

Chris Papple, Alexandre and Debbie Gabriel, Richard Bates and James Cherry, and Pete, Sophie, Olga, Ben and the entire Union Club team. Lastly to our families: Vic Grier, Caroline Ridley and Lois and Honor for being super supportive and telling us if the drinks were tasty... or not!

Cheers!
Kampai!
Prost!
Santé!
Skål!
Sláinte!

Index

Published in North
America in 2022 by
Princeton Architectural Press
70 West 36th Street
New York, NY 10018
www.papress.com

First published in
Great Britain in 2022 by
Mitchell Beazley,
an imprint of Octopus
Publishing Group Ltd
Carmelite House
50 Victoria Embankment
London EC4Y 0DZ
www.octopusbooks.co.uk

An Hachette UK Company
www.hachette.co.uk

Printed and bound in China
25 24 23 22 4 3 2 1 First edition

ISBN 978-1-64896-176-2

Library of Congress Control
Number: 2022934637

For Mitchell Beazley
Group Publishing Director:
    Denise Bates
Creative Director:
    Jonathan Christie
Senior Editor: Pauline Bache
Copyeditor: Jo Richardson
Photographer:
    Vinny Whiteman
Prop stylist: Sarah Birks
Mixologist: Missy Flynn
Senior Production Manager:
    Peter Hunt

For Princeton
Architectural Press
Editor: Holly La Due
Cover Design: Paul Wagner

**All cocktail recipes serve one
unless otherwise stated.**

**All parts refer to a
standard cocktail measure:
1 fl oz or 25 ml.**

About the authors

Neil Ridley (left) and Joel Harrison (right) are award-winning drinks writers, presenters and broadcasters who have to-date written six books, winning the 'Best Drinks Book' at the Fortnum & Mason Food and Drink Awards along the way. The pair write for a range of newspapers and magazines, and appear regularly as drinks experts on Channel 4's *Sunday Brunch*.